D0366946

DATE DUE

THE
ELEMENTS
OF D8ING

THE
ELEMENTS
OF D8ING

THE ESSENTIAL LGBTQ GUIDE TO MEETING, CONNECTING, DATING, AND LOVING

TYE FARLEY and TOSIN ADESANYA

of d8ablellc.com

Skyhorse Publishing

Skyhorse Publishing books may be purchased in bulk at special discounts for sales promotion, corporate gifts, fund-raising, or educational purposes. Special editions can also be created to specifications. For details, contact the Special Sales Department, Skyhorse Publishing, 307 West 36th Street, 11th Floor, New York, NY 10018or info@skyhorsepublishing.com.

Skyhorse® and Skyhorse Publishing® are registered trademarks of Skyhorse Publishing, Inc.®, a Delaware corporation.

Visit our website at www.skyhorsepublishing.com.

10 9 8 7 6 5 4 3 2 1

306.730866 FAR

Library of Congress Cataloging-in-Publication Data is available on file.

Cover design by Philip Price at PPGFX

Print ISBN: 978-1-5107-1281-2
Ebook ISBN: 978-1-5107-1282-9

Printed in the United States of America

Contents

CHAPTER 1

THE SUPERFICIAL GAY: INTIMACY

SELF, APPRECIATION, COMMON INTERESTS, REASONABLE EXPECTATIONS

We are visual creatures. There's no way around this fact. Without getting too deep into the biological jargon, the placement of our eyes is the result of thousands of years of evolution . . . And for what, exactly? They are the first judges of any given scenario. Sight is, more often than not, the first sense that wakes up your brain so you can recognize those potential life-changing moments. You know, those times when you may need to fight, those times when you need to run your ass off . . . and those promising times when you want to get some serious fucking done.

Yes, the so-called windows to our respective souls know what we want before the brain even realizes it. Let's set the scene. You're in a dimly lit lounge. The thickness of the dark is penetrated only with the occasional jab of light from the fixtures above. Teasingly, the light washes across the face of a veritable specimen. They were visible only for a second, but that second was all your eyes needed to slap the pleasure center of your brain. Now, maybe you're naturally the outgoing type. Maybe it's the orgy of beats and sound intertwined with the marriage of your eighteen-year-old whiskey, ice, and lime. Whatever your starting block, the endgame is the same. You want what you see and you're going to make that play to get what you want, because no hot and sweaty encounter has ever occurred without those eyes of yours okaying it first. Then everything else falls into place, right?

Right?

Who doesn't like running their fingers down a set of abs that would make Adonis want to renew his gym membership? Would you complain about big, defined arms that could otherwise manhandle a bench press if they weren't currently pinning you against the wall, only to follow up by forcefully introducing you to that California King mattress? What about a set of lips that would make Angelina—no, Marilyn Monroe—one jealous girl? Lips that you know could suck the polish off a . . . But, ahem, let's not digress.

Because we're initially visually stimulated, and because attraction, for the most part, starts with what we see, then it's not hard to believe that a certain level of superficiality has to exist in order for attraction to be present. As a matter of fact, one could argue that without superficiality, preferences wouldn't exist. If we couldn't distinguish between who we thought was smoking hot and whom we considered to be fifteen seconds in the microwave, would there even be a desire to go after anyone?

Yes, we need to be superficial on some level.

But, as they say, too much of anything can be detrimental. Many times, we allow what someone looks like to govern the path we take with that person. If all you're into is meeting and bedding as many hot bodies as you can find, then by all means, let superficiality run your social life. There will be no need to dig deeper. There will be no reason to get to know someone on any plane other than the physical one. Why waste your time? You're better off objectifying. You're better off locking your emotions up tight. You're better off dismissing the possibility of building the rock-solid bridge needed to create, grow, and sustain a healthy relationship because you're more interested in testing the durability of your bedsprings.

The absolute truth is, visual stimulation will get you only so far. It's just enough to set the beginning stages for the foundation of a potential relationship. Think of it as the gateway drug to more . . . if you want more.

For those who want more, read on.

You've met this weekend's Mona Lisa. For all intents and purposes, the object you have in front of you is the visage of beauty incarnate . . . for the weekend, or maybe even just tonight. But make no mistake, this person at this point is nothing more than an object. How could they be anything more? You just met them. Even if you exchange numbers and engage in the typical alcohol-induced verbiage, you haven't even begun to scratch the tip of the tip of who they are. Hell, you probably haven't even taken them to the bedroom for the horizontal salsa session.

Let's slow it down, take a step back. You've reached the first of many crossroads that all potential relationships reach. Regardless of whether you met your potential love interest at Whole Foods, or a shadowy, rhythmic sweatbox, your brain immediately begins to decide exactly what part this character will play in your life story (even though we tend to erroneously assume that just because we met them shaking their ass, they can't be a viable candidate for the long term).

Categorization is the name of the game. We all do it. We immediately begin to assess exactly where someone will fit into our lives as soon as we meet them. The scenario in which we've met them, the clothes they wear—even the way we've observed their interaction with others plays a part in determining exactly what role this person will play in our lives. "She'll be a good friend." "He's fun to hang out and drink with." "I don't like her; she talks too damned much." The same thing goes for potential intimate relationships.

We typically place folks in one of three interconnected categories, which are held together by transitional phases. Please see the ubercomplex visual setup below that represents the progression/regression of intimate relationship development:

Imagine the white space just to the left of the figure as your starting point. This is the time right before you notice someone you're physically attracted to. The line where the white space meets the first rectangle shape represents the time period during which your superficial self takes over, followed immediately by the first rapport-building moment. This is promptly followed by the initial phase in the dating process, which is assessing if someone is worthy of being

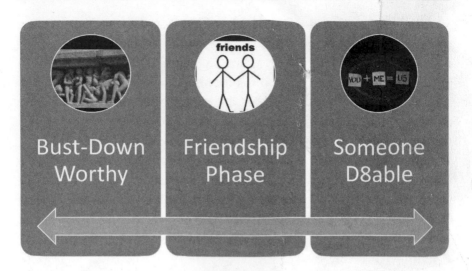

romped. The white spaces represent rapport-building opportunities for the different stages. The other two rectangles represent the respective ranges for friendship and dating. Finally, the double-sided arrow represents the possibility of a potential love interest moving between the three dating ranges, which is dependent upon your experience with that person.

Confused yet?

Well, let's look at, in theory, how we go about mentally labeling those people we have an intimate interest in. In order to do that, we have to reexamine superficiality. At this point, we're sure you have come to accept the fact that a level of superficiality is needed in attraction. Maybe it's because the aforementioned explanation pertaining to superficiality made perfect sense to you. Or, it could be that, for once, being labeled as a superficial individual isn't all that bad. Either way, it is understood that a certain level of snobbishness as it relates to physical attraction is necessary, and being a dick is arguably a biological imperative on some level.

The Catalyst: Superficial Spark

It would be wrong to refer to this particular part of your relationship journey as a phase, but it is important nonetheless. The Superficial

Spark is the catalyst, if you will, that jump-starts the chain reaction that may lead to a relationship. Think of this portion of your journey as the flame from a match that lights a stick of dynamite. The Superficial Spark is the exact moment you see someone whom you're attracted to and the immediate actions that follow. This is the point that alters your view of a particular person. It separates them from the masses of folks you wouldn't think twice about. It also alters the way you interact with that person as you mentally prepare to pursue the new object of your potential affections. You assign a higher level of importance to people you're attracted to. Don't believe it? Ask yourself if you've ever been nervous interacting with someone you perceived to be unattractive. Nope, because what they think about you doesn't matter to you anyway.

Have you ever been to a huge social gathering and run across someone so hot, the rest of the people don't really matter all that much? Of course you have. Most, if not all, of us have been in a scenario similar to this. Your brain creates a hierarchy of hotness. You've got dude number one who looks like the love child of Brad Pitt and Denzel Washington. Guy number two may be a Shemar Moore look-alike . . . etc., etc. You, without even thinking about it, have listed all the people you're attracted to. At this point, that Superficial Spark has primed you to deal with that list of people.

The next step is the total objectification of the person you're attracted to. Settle down, you're not a bad person just because you break someone, whom you don't know, down to a set of attractive limbs, a killer torso, and full, fleshy lips. If they weren't a prime piece of meat, in your mind, you wouldn't be considering tasting the goods in the first place. Chalk it up to the fight-flight-or-fuck assessment mentioned earlier. It's natural. It should also be noted that the Superficial Spark phase, in general, is a relatively quick process. This is because, at this point, you don't have anything substantial to go on other than physical appearance. "This girl is gorgeous, and these are the reasons why . . ." Period. Seriously, if the first thing you think of when you glance at a new sexy is their views on the global economy, or how they feel about dancing in the rain, you have the makings of a stalker . . . or a stage-seven cling master.

After your favorable assessment is complete, which can take any-where from three to five seconds, you shift into hunting mode. Not every hunter's tactics are the same, but every single one of us has an approach . . . or a non-approach. We all have some way to attempt to garner attention from the person we're interested in.

But wait . . .

You didn't assume that this is a one-way street, did you? The entire time you've been eye-sexing a potential boy toy, you better believe that, if he accepts your advances, Mr. Male Model has already given you the ocular dick-down himself. That's right. People have already run your visual application through their respective nocturnal playtime data-bases to see if you have the potential to hold the playmate position. You should also realize that *you are not* the only applicant, just as they aren't your only interest at this point in the game.

If both sides agree (which is essentially mutually favorable visual stimulation), then the first bridge has been reached.

Just the Tip or Before-the-Sheets Prerequisite

The first bridge you'll have to cross on your journey, or first rapport-building stage, is the game of question and answer you'll play when you initially interview that potential playmate. Make no mistake, this first conversation is an interview even if you're screaming over deep-house beats and drowning in vodka. It is a form of verbal cat-and-mouse, if you will. Think of these transitional periods as time for data collec-tion. The information you gather, along with your superficial visual stimulation—and frankly, how horny you are—will determine what you (want to) do with this person next.

This exchange of words is staged for two reasons.

Firstly, the two of you are attempting to figure out if you can stand each other, not to get along for anything deep or substantial at this point. No, no, no, you two already like what you see. This dialogue, lightly seasoned with libido and a dash of humor, is simply used as a testing agent. If you guys hit it off, then your visual stimulation is for-tified with the idea that the new cutie is at least cool enough to twist around in the bedroom. If, for whatever reason, you guys bomb at the pre-sex checker game . . . you may still engage in a bout of hate sex. More likely than not, however, you guys will go your separate ways, no matter how fine the candidate is.

Secondly, a simple conversation lessens the feel of total streetwalkerdom. People do dirt. People like to do dirt. They just don't want to be seen as dirty. It is not acceptable to walk into a bar, grunt, and point at whom you want. If it were, you can be sure there would be no need for this manual. You can also blame the unfair stigma attached to one-night stands on a hypocritical, judgmental society, but it does look better if you engage in a simple conversation before walking out with someone you just met.

Upon completion of the initial interview, the candidate is placed somewhere within the first range of the developmental process of relationship establishment to await further evaluation. In other words, you guys like each other enough, at the very least, to get naked together and discuss the birds and bees and such. That initial conversation, however, does kind of determine where within the first category your new interest may fall. For example, if the two of you barely manage to pull each other's names past the onslaught of dirty martinis, you may subconciously place the candidate closer to the beginning stages of the Bust-Down category. They may fall somewhere between One-Hit Wonder and your Once a Month, Thursday Afternoon. If, however, you two really seem to hit it off, your new acquaintance could very well be placed closer to the following transitional period and sub-range: Friendship . . . somewhere near Fuck-Buddy Specialist.

If cupid is feeling extraordinarily generous and decides to shoot hollow-pointed arrows up your ass, and you two really hit it off, you could very well speed your candidate through the bust-down phase altogether. You'll end up in the second transitional phase (which we will touch on later).

It should also be noted that not everyone's internal clock is the same. Just because you're smitten after the first three minutes doesn't mean that the other person is, or vice versa. Fairy tales are just that: stories.

They are the exception to the norm. Love at first sight tends to happen only with people and their favorite meals. Take that into account as things start to progress.

Being Bust-Down Worthy

Ah yes, category number one. How do we begin to explain the categories and how someone transitions through them? The best way to envision intimate growth between two people is to imagine the first category, Bust-Down Worthy, to be the first plateau in a series of plateaus that need to be climbed in order to reach D8able status. Within this plateau is a series of mini plateaus, or person-specific stages, that your potential love interest will traverse on the way to being with you in a committed relationship.

The figure below is a good example:

Within the initial Bust-Down Worthy category, your viewpoint of the person you're seeing may mirror the example above. As you may recall, it's not that you're devaluing the person, but rather that all you know about them at this stage is that they're attractive . . . and thoughts of sexual games dance across your mind because of it. This isn't a bad thing. It's natural because the limited information you received during your first interaction is all you have to go on. And what is that information?

A. They're hot.
B. They don't annoy you so much that you wouldn't bother having sex with them.

If this is as far as you want to take them, then so be it. There's no need to explore any further. Truthfully, some people won't get any further than this particular plateau anyway, simply because you're not going to be compatible on a higher level. You may not even be compatible on this level, but as of right now, you guys have a mutual physical attraction.

Well, how does one get out of the dungeons of your mind and into the penthouse of your thoughts? To put it simply, through actions and information. The more favorable information you receive that is fortified by favorable action, the more that person is able to cross those mini plateaus. Of course, "favorable" is a relative term. The things you love about someone could be the same things that others find loathsome, depraved, and sick. Not everyone enjoys road-head, nor does everyone enjoy a prude, shoulda-joined-the-monastery kind of individual.

When you're interacting with someone, on an intimate level or otherwise, you're constantly pulling information from that person. This info clues you in on how to deal with that person. For instance, you've learned that your boss is a crab-ass at the end of the month, so you've modified your behavior to better handle the stick that grows in his rear every thirty days. In dealing with affairs of an intimate nature, the way you take and use the information gathered is slightly different. You internalize everything you learn. You make judgments based on your preferences, morals, beliefs, etc. In the case of your boss, you don't really have a say in what goes on. You either deal and adapt, or update that LinkedIn account. In the case of a potential Portia de Rossi to your Ellen, you can decide whether or not you want to deal with that person. Whether or not you realize it, during the early dating phases, you're constantly evaluating what you do and don't like about your love interest. This info determines exactly where they'll end up in your life.

So, someone has successfully made it to the Bust-Down Worthy stage. Their actions and the information you gather will determine whether they make it to the next stage. How does this happen? Well, keep in mind the duality of your interactions with this person. You're not only receiving information from them but also sharing who you are as well. When thoughts, feelings, experiences, physical attraction, and a whole host of other elements are congruent, rapport is developed. The more time you spend with someone, the more information you gather, and the stronger a rapport becomes . . . if the other person's information and actions are harmonious with your own. The amount of time for the development of rapport is not universal for all relationships, but the gathering and processing of information happens in all intimate scenarios. Get it?

The real reason most dating experts will advise against getting down to the get-down too soon (while someone is in the bust-down stage) is because you've built only a rapport at this point, which is conducive to sex. Thus, arguably, you don't have enough of a foundation to build anything else on.

The only way, if that's what you want, to transition out of the Bust-Down Worthy stage with someone is to allow enough time to gather and process the information to do so. This is not to say that you two couldn't mutually dickmatize each other in love, but more often than not, your superficial attraction and Bust-Down information are not enough to grow and sustain a lasting relationship.

Getting stymied in the Bust-Down stage is an issue that isn't the easiest to rectify. This is why your actions during this period are so weighty. Remember, the other person does not have much information on your character to go on at this point. Unfortunately, your actions are it. So, if you fuck on the first date, there's a significant chance that your playmate will drop you into *that* category. And what's worse is that they'll probably assume that you're like that with everyone. Now, it could be that the stars were aligned. Maybe the chemistry between you two was amazing and natural, like oxygen and two hydrogen atoms. But relying on the other person to realize it was utter magic that you two ended up naked right away is not a great idea.

Show some restraint, and your potential partner will thank you for it later. Humans are reactionary creatures. Present yourself in a respectful way, and your partner has to respect you. If not, they get the boot early. Making someone wait for the tail isn't about teasing them. It's strictly about giving them more time to see more of you as an individual. If that eventually bombs, then you still get to sleep with them . . .

When You Like Someone (Pre-Friendship) . . .

Here's the major indicator that the gap between the Bust-Down and Friendship stages is about to be filled. The things you learn—and crave to learn about your wannabe cuddle buddy—start to change. They take on more depth. You'll notice that you won't be so focused on the superficial things. Sure, you'll still want to sully the bedsheets, but you'll be interested in learning higher-plane things about this person. Common interests will bring you closer together. You have now reached the second rapport-building stage. You're well on your way to ushering your new interest into the ever-important Friendship category.

During this transitional phase, your focus shifts to learning things about your love interest that don't just deal with their appearance. As a matter of fact, once you've made up your mind to try to find out more about this person, you subconciously move toward learning more of the things that affect them on a mental level. What you do with this type of information ultimately determines what you want for the future of your relationship with them.

Have you ever wondered what the difference between a player and everyone else is? With affairs of the heart, everyone pretty much starts out the same. We all have a system of gathering and evaluating information on the person we're interested in. When you reach the Pre-Friendship transitional phase, both people involved have attained a mutual level of comfort. They're readily sharing intimate details about their lives in a subconcious attempt to decide whether or not the other person is a potential love match. It is what people do with the information gathered during the Pre-Friendship phase that determines their intentions, thusly separating player-types from other folks.

Those who use the intimate details obtained from one another for selfish, personal gain at this stage—in any shape, form, or fashion—are player-types. Yeah, being a player doesn't just mean weaseling sexual playtime out of someone. It can also entail manipulating intimate details to construct a fake bond in order to obtain, well, anything you're looking to get out of someone. Those who gather these details in the hope of developing an altruistic and intimate bond with someone are the people trying to build a real relationship. Either way, the Pre-Friendship phase is the time period when this is typically done. It is up to you to decide which road to take.

The Pre-Friendship Phase Model can be imagined like so:

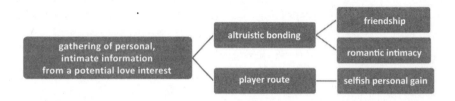

As you can see from the spiffy model provided, the initial corralling of intimate details is the same, whether you're a player or a genuine person trying to build something. In true relationship building, your rapport is strengthened as your love interest's life experiences mirror or complement your own. The more commonalities you have, like world-view, an interest in traveling, and other personality-building elements, the stronger of a bond that can be forged. The differences you and your love interest may have can also be an intriguing lure and pull you closer together, because they'll increase your chances of exploring new things together (this will be discussed later).

There are two possible routes to real altruistic bonding. You may find that the person you're spending time with and learning about has the physical and mental attractiveness you need in order to pursue a relationship with them. On the other hand, you could just end up with a very attractive friend. It is not out of the realm of possibility that, after learning more about this person, you two actually fit better as friends. And hot friends have hot friends . . .

Because relationship building is a two-way street, and you're making yourself vulnerable as well, it would be beneficial for you to know how to spot player tendencies earlier in the game. The Pre-Friendship phase is the rapport-building transitional period that determines into what plateau in the Friendship category your budding love interest will fall.

So, spotting the player indicators now, or at least red-flagging potential player activity, will save you the headaches later on. As a rule of thumb, at the core of every player is the drive to get what they want through selfish actions. They may seem nice, sweet, and even caring at times, but their core is that of staunch egocentric intent. In other words, you both have internal timetables and motivation. If you find yourself constantly adhering to the other person's timetable to do things too soon (be it having sex too soon, spending money on them too soon, etc.), there is a chance that you're dealing with an egocentrist . . . or at the least, a selfish asshole. While one red flag isn't enough to crucify someone, you can't play the Jesus role and forgive them for a multitude of sins.

And Then There Was Friendship

The definition of friendship is merely a mutual affection or mutual affinity between two or more people. So it is not hard to understand why the Friendship phase in dating is so elastic, so convoluted. People can have a mutual affection for each other in a multitude of ways that don't even include the dating world. You can have friends you drink with. You can have friends who are there only to travel with. You can have friends who will sleep with you when the two of you aren't tied down, and some who won't give a shit if you're in dating confinement. Some people consider their hairdressers friends, even if they simply touch up the do every now and again.

For the purposes of dating, we will steer clear of any platonic affinities. When the terms "friendship" and "friend" are used, they are referring to the elastic, intermediate mush that is the gooey center of the dating and relationship sandwich. There isn't a pretty little diagram that can accurately portray how someone advances through the Friendship stage. Yes, there are plateaus. Yes, there is still the continuation of gathering and evaluating intimate details about the other person. But—and it's a huge but—the friendship progression is far from linear. You could jump from one plateau to another, slide down a few stairs, climb a ladder or two, and even end up back where you started. Imagine Super Mario Brothers in 3-D, and you start to get the feel of navigating the Friendship phase.

In a perfect world, two people meet. They're physically attracted to one another, and come to find out that they possess a mental and life experience familiarity as well. They begin dating exclusively, fall in love, get hitched, get the dog and the white picket fence, and live happily ever after.

In the real world, however, relationship development is far more subconsciously involved. This is because you're not only learning about the person you're interested in, you're also learning about yourself. That, and you're also evolving. You are the sum of all your emotions and experiences, and people tend to apply that sum to their new dating equations. Ushering someone through the Friendship phase is based so much on personal preference and experience that no person's journey is the same. Not only that, but you won't assess any of your potential love interests in the same way. Sharon may remind you of Rhonda, your ex. Because of that, your previous experience may dictate how you treat Sharon. Certain people you may lock on to faster than others. Some you may realize are better as friends than as potential lovers. Let's not forget Superficiality constantly bugging you, constantly pushing you to do things that you may not be ready for, constantly reminding you of how big her breasts are, how defined her squat-infused ass is.

On the flip side of the coin, the new monopolizing object of your thoughts will be running you through their past experiences and cascade of emotions as well. The Friendship phase can be a huge game of emotional Frogger.

At its very foundation, the Friendship phase is like a weed-out course at a higher education institution. You're not just able to act on impulse and emotion here; you're proactively going to push forward. Before you can graduate to the next transitional phase, you're going to have to take an honest look at yourself and what you want. You're going to have to get rid of the elements of yourself that no longer have a place. Superficiality is definitely going to have to take a back seat because, in order to develop a real relationship, you're going to have to be just as attracted to the mentally confidential portion of the person as well as the sexy wrapping. You'll also need to learn how to take someone as the total package they are, meaning they'll have things about them you'll love, and certain things you could definitely live without.

You'll know when you've reached the threshold for the final transitional phase, the Pre-D8able bridge. The fluidity and convolution of the Friendship phase will become rigid. A prime candidate would have survived your mental minefield and still be standing, and would probably appear more attractive than when they got through the Bust-Down Worthy phase. You'll be ready to move on once you've targeted which person stands above the rest. They're hot, they possess elements other than sexual ones that pique your interest, and you're beginning to think that they have enough to offer to keep you from looking elsewhere. But how, just how, can you guys make the switch from hot friends to two people who are exclusively D8able?

The Pre-D8

There's a certain Al Pacino character from a certain movie who compares love and sex to consuming large quantities of chocolate. There are studies that claim love can't be definitively explained. It should be no shocker then that it's a veritable impossibility to calculate the exact moment a special friend reaches the D8able threshold. The truth is that every scenario is different and people reach these Eureka moments at different times. Even within a relationship, one person may be a go while the other one is still in the evaluating stages. There's no right answer here.

There are a few things you can certainly avoid, however. Once you've reached the point where you really consider dating someone, do a little bit of soul-searching. Make sure you reached this point on your own. Yeah, sure you wouldn't be considering this course if the other person involved didn't give you reasons to do so, but make sure the other person didn't push you into it.

Secondly, don't trick yourself into dating someone if you're not ready. "Well, she's probably the best I can do," or "I'm not getting any younger." Screw that way of thinking. Don't settle on a shaky situation. If you're questioning your feelings, you're definitely standing on an active fault line and need to take a step back. A wise person once said that if someone has to evaluate a yes-or-no situation, then in that current place, the answer is no. If you're still on the fence, then no may be the best way to go at the time. There's no sense in wasting your time or the other person's. It's better to step back than be flaky.

Once you've ultimately decided to pursue a relationship with the object of your affections, communication will be central to all things. Communication has always been important, but at this juncture of your relationship and going forward, dialogue is like the air you breathe. Because both of you are agreeing to go forward with this dating thing, there can't be any gray area. You need to know what your partner wants and needs, and they need to do the same. There are no guarantees with anything, but you can greatly strengthen your chances of dating success by being open and honest with the new boo, and most importantly yourself. No, this isn't some cryptic piece of advice you'd see in some corner-store magazine. Before you two agree to D8, you should eliminate, on both sides, as many potential negative surprises as possible. This means not pretending to be okay with any of your boo's negative behavior patterns now, only to use those same patterns against them five months later. Get all the bullshit out now.

When it's all said and done, you'll find yourself ready to be D8able.

Being D8able

Once the two of you have consciously made the decision to date each other, your best friend will be time. At this point, you already know you like each other. You've either explored each other in the bedroom or are well on your way to beginning that adventure. You guys are walking around with that new-relationship smell. It smells a lot like expensive wine, carnival cotton candy, fresh linen, and the adventure of the unknown.

But time reveals all things.

You don't make the decision to date only to let your relationship die out. Relationships should be treated like living, breathing things. They need to be fed with the exploration of common interests and the sharing of differences to create new adventure. Getting settled in is the worst way to kill the relationship before it gets going. As a matter of fact, settling in can kill a relationship at any stage. It will take two pro-active participants to foster a relationship that is mutually beneficial to both. As a basic guideline to nurturing a relationship, just remember this:

Relationships work best when you put the other person's needs and wants ahead of your own. The other person in turn should always do the same for you. If done correctly, neither one of you will ever feel the want for anything more, because your needs and wants are covered by the very person whose needs and wants you're taking care of. You're creating a sort of self-sustaining, ever-evolving, little bubble universe, where you two are the only inhabitants.

Don't allow the relationship to get stale, and it won't die out. The things you did to catch someone should be the foundation with which you build new structures to keep them there, and to keep them happy.

Similar to the previous stages, the D8able stage is a lot like a series of escalating plateaus. It may look something like this in your mind:

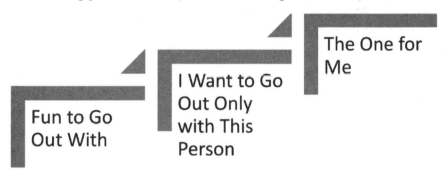

Fun to Go Out With

I Want to Go Out Only with This Person

The One for Me

Remember, time is your best friend. The more you spend (time, that is), the more you get to know about this person, mentally, physically, socially, everything. If you guys take the aforementioned guideline and really try to apply it to your budding relationship, you'll progress through the D8able plateaus pretty easily. Of course, no one is perfect, and you'll probably have to navigate through some rocky terrain every now and then, but the strength in your relationship will be drawn from the ability to be each other's support systems.

Who knows, the thoroughbred you just wanted to saddle up could end up having the very pedigree you needed to get you out of the pastures. Hopefully, this manual keeps you from blindly navigating the stormy, choppy waters we all know dating can be.

Things to Consider

Superficiality.

You thought we were done here, didn't you? Not a chance. We've discussed, extensively, the reasons a certain level of superficial thinking . . . attraction . . . whatever . . . is not necessarily a bad thing. However, too much of anything is not a good thing. As a matter of fact, too many times, people will allow the superficial portions of themselves to govern their actions, clouding their thought processes. You've heard statements like this: "She's so hot, she can get away with being a bitch." "He's so fine, he deserves to be a player." Ummm, no. They don't have the right to treat other people like shit just because they're physically attractive. That's the superficial part of you that is sending you into numbskullsville.

Too much shallowness in one's mind tends to elevate the aspects of others that really don't matter all that much.

The superficial elements of your being are rooted in emotion and visual stimulation. Left unchecked, these elements can poison your mind, leading you to look at the world ass-backward. You cannot allow superficiality to go any further than where it should: for initial attraction. Allowing emotion to run through you, unchecked, is like a stampede of bulls demolishing a small town as they rush through it.

Common sense is the first thing to be utterly obliterated. Ask yourself this: Do you want to find a meaningful relationship? Do you want someone to explore the world with? Do you want to find that person worth exploring, the person you want to explore you? Do you want someone to see you for the whole, good person you think you are? If you've answered yes to any of these questions, how could you think, in the slightest, that the superficial route would be the way to go when trying to develop a relationship filled with love, mutual respect, and longevity?

Superficiality does not deal with the weighty, substantial portions of people that actually make them people. In the grand scheme of things, does his six-pack guarantee happiness and satisfaction in a relationship? Will her great ass get you through the tough times at work? It may, ahem, help you to forget about the tough times for a while . . . but gazing at her booty won't fix the problems. Only her caring side can give you the support you need during those times. But how would you even know if she has that side to her if you're more worried about her hair than her heart?

In all honesty, this shallow, vapid way of judging people is dysfunctional at best once you've decided to progress past the Bust-Down Worthy stage. The human being is made up in equal parts of brain power and emotion. The brain keeps the emotions from running wild, when you use it. Emotions and feelings are there to keep you from turning into a cold-hearted robot. There's a healthy balance you need to achieve. Allowing your superficial side to take over is basically you willfully forfeiting all the pieces of a mate you need to be happy other than the aesthetically pleasing outer shell. We need emotional and mental stimulation and nurturing to achieve happiness and satisfaction within an intimate union.

Do yourself a favor: think clearly and in balance when it comes to matters of the heart. Just because the guy doesn't totally match some mental laundry list of physical characteristics you'd like, it doesn't mean he's not a good fit for you. Who gives a shit if he's five feet nine inches when he's willing to make you feel ten feet tall? Make decisions and take action with your heart in mind, but don't allow your heart to control those decisions.

Dating . . .

Dating is not rigid. We've created the model to better illustrate how people progress through the stages of dating. It does not, however, take into account many peripheral elements that can and often do affect someone's progression. For example, time is an extremely relative aspect that affects everyone differently. You may be the person who falls in love right away, while your friend could move at a snail's pace.

You know by this time how superficiality can move people through the stages and sub-plateaus, sometimes even when they shouldn't move at all.

Things like proximity and rate of exposure also play important roles in attraction and will be discussed in later chapters.

Also, and probably most importantly, the dating model doesn't address people's ability to slide backward. The dating game is a lot like a complicated chess match because of all the internal elements that affect people on an individual basis, as well as the bordering aspects. No two people view the world completely the same and this fact is at its most evident in the dating realm. The guy you were smitten with yesterday could be a cold fish today. The selfish jerk you thought you were falling for could've hung herself in a lie.

All that being said, people can backtrack. We are a whirlwind of emotions and feelings and needs and wants. We can make mistakes. We can hurt, and we can be hurt. Contrarily, someone who you thought was only Bust-Down Worthy could totally surprise you, show you another side of them, and end up knocking on D8able's door. The point is, just because someone has reached a certain plateau doesn't mean they'll stay there. You are in no way protected from potential pain no matter how you try to prepare, just as you can't hide from love if Cupid decides to force-feed you his arrows.

Your best bet is to focus on you, really learn about yourself, and be better prepared to handle the roller coaster we all know as dating. This will definitely be discussed later on in the manual.

CHAPTER 2

FIVE-DATE RULE

TRUST, RESPECT, APPRECIATION

The battle between the big brain and little brain has been going on since the dawn of man. The moment we found out how good it felt to stimulate our respective nether regions, with that certain rhythm, the big brain was waving the white flag. One could argue that the moment we learned of self-gratification—masturbation for the laymen—we focused our energies on finding different, more satisfying ways to lose some baby juice. We had to up the ante for every orgasm.

To put it simply, your baby-making parts are a gateway drug. Well, they are your primary tool for everyone's favorite drug, sex. Like other controlled substances, they tend to make your brain function rather abnormally when under their influence. That's putting it lightly. When you're enduring a dick-overdose or a coochie-coma, your playtime pieces are clouding your judgment to such a severe degree that common sense may as well turn in its resignation.

Have you ever looked at those drug addict mugshots online or in the newspaper? Or have you ever had to witness the transition in mental focus of those who get addicted to drugs? At first the drug is just a recreational thing, which eventually evolves into something incorporated into the user's way of life. Ultimately, the thing that started out as a want becomes an uncontrollable need that eats away at the very makeup of an addict.

And so can the want for sex . . .

You may not look like an extra from *The Walking Dead* because you crave sexual stimulation all of the time, but the similarities between the way we progress from casual sexual stimulation to our unbridled need for it are damn near parallel to the transition from recreational drug user to needled-up, glass-dick junky. When you first discover masturbation, the sexual gratification is foreign to you but you know you like it. The same goes for initially using a hard drug. The feeling is foreign to you, but you're drawn to it. As time progresses, you become used to the sensation, maybe even slightly desensitized. So what happens next? You've got to find a new way—a better way—to enhance the sensation. With drug users it's all about finding the next more powerful high. In terms of sex and gratification, it's about achieving a more body-rocking orgasm.

Why the similarities, and why is this so important?

The human brain processes pleasure the same way, no matter the origin. One word: dopamine. Be it eating food you like, snorting a line of cocaine, or having the biggest testicle-draining orgasm of your life, dopamine is involved. Dopamine, in short, is located in specific regions of your brain that control pleasure. It acts as a messenger, telling your body when to feel pleasure. Things like drugs and sex act as catalysts that release the dopamine in your system, causing you to feel the pleasure from being high or the pleasure from sexual release. Over time, your body gets used to dopamine being released through the same actions over and over again, causing you to have to find different, more powerful ways to get that rush.

Now granted, controlled substances have a much more detrimental effect on your overall health and brain function, but the pleasure you seek to receive from sexual acts can cloud your brain just as smoking a joint can make your decisions foggy. The repeated acquisition of pleasure from sexual acts trains your brain to want it more and more. So is it any wonder that at this point in your life, the little brain can win in a match of wits against its bigger brother? Little B has been getting the older brother stone-cold high the entire time.

You Need a Moment of Clarity

Because we are sexual beings, and because we've conditioned our-selves all the way down to the chemical level to seek out sexual pleasure, clearing the fog in our respective brains can be difficult. Couple the orgasm-saturated, endorphin-seeking pleasure centers of a sex-hazed mind with the superficiality involved in initial attraction, and it's a wonder monogamous relationships even exist within our species. Just as a quick recap, recall that initial attraction is spurred by superficial visual stimulation (see Chapter 1). This is the time period, in essence, where you totally objectify the person you're eye-ing. "Damn, he's got nice arms. Wow, I bet those abs and shoulders could . . ." It's almost like being at a Vegas buffet and you haven't eaten in days. Your brain and your body are craving an endorphin release.

If you have sex on the brain, and most of us usually do, seeing that hot specimen across the room is going to exponentially amplify your want (which your brain is categorizing as a *need* because sex weighs heavily on the mind) to plug your dick into something snug, damp, and inviting . . . especially if the aforementioned specimen *is* in fact inviting you. Your penis is a loaded rifle, and you'd like nothing more than to hunt down and fire a few rounds into the cutie with the big, brown, woodland-creature-like eyes in front of you.

This may not be the best idea, especially if you're the relationship type.

Thinking with the Little Brain

Even when it's aroused and fully aware, the baby brain isn't all that smart. Baby brain, or Little B, as it likes to be called in a formal setting, is never going to be able to figure out complex equations. It'll never be able to process what you're reading here. It has a one-track mind: sex. Little B focuses so much on that one thought, that it is able to sway the bigger, smarter, more capable brother into making dumb decisions all for the sake of the next fling. Little B believes in getting down, and then getting down some more.

Fucking early and often usually leads to more fucking early and often. Remember, when you don't allow yourself enough time to get to know someone, and vice versa, you don't have much to go on other than the fact that the two of you are attracted to each other. There's nothing there to add to the initial Superficial Spark. When there's nothing else to add, the only option we have, as humans, is the want to have sex because the entire basis of the attraction at this point is visual stimulation. This is why the initial stage in relationship building is known as the Bust-Down Worthy stage, because all you know at this point is that sex can be had with the person in front of you. Be honest with yourself. Have you ever laid eyes on someone and wondered what museums they like to visit? Hell no. You may have thought about getting naughty behind the Picasso exhibit at the museum . . . but that's only if you first saw the person at the museum.

Realize that your target probably has you in their scope too. Also make the realization that seduction—good seduction—is magnetic as a motherfucker. And there's nothing more seductive than two people vibing at the right place, *even if it ain't the right time*.

The scene could be set perfectly. The music is right. The lighting is right. The alcohol could be tongue-kissing your thoughts, convincing you that going home with *this* hottie is . . . the . . . perfect . . . idea. Your little brain is in agreement, and the big one is down for the count. Furthermore, your new friend's mental team isn't going to fight the rhythm you two are generating. They do this on a weekly basis with people just like you. That Little B is in control of that team. At the moment, you don't seem to mind your respective genitalia negotiating for the two of you.

But, stop. Make the affirmation that you're worth more. Believe that you're worth more. Show that you're worth more. The Bust-Down Worthy stage is a destination that can be revisited once you guys have explored more of the respective road maps of who you are.

The Sex-First Fallacy

We live in an "I want it now" society. If you don't know the answer to something, you can Google it. We have phones in our pockets that may as well be mini supercomputers. There's an application for anything and everything. We can shop online. We can book travel with the help of an Ethernet cable. You can get a hold of any porn you're into, instantly. We all know about dating online. Smart TVs. You name it; we've probably got a way to get it, and rather quickly. We have been conditioned for instant gratification. Getting sexual playtime has never been as easy as it is right now, and it'll probably continue to get easier.

Just because it's easy, and just because it's on everyone's mind, doesn't mean that having sex right away is the best idea.

What are some of the misconceptions we have about getting the deed done early? Well, one falsehood is the thought that getting the freak done early can weed out the bad lovers. If he sucks in bed, there's no need to keep him around after the first one or two rounds in the sack.

Sure, no one wants to buy a car without test-driving it. But similar to a car, your value will depreciate if you allow someone to strap up in your driver's seat too soon. But, we're all human, and we all have urges. How realistic is it to hold off on sex before monogamy? People love to pretend that sex isn't an important element in a relationship. But that's all it is, pretend. Sex, along with a mental and maybe even a spiritual connection, works in unison to bring people closer to their mates. So, sex cannot be ignored, as it is a valuable factor in deciding whether or not a relationship has staying power.

But . . .

It's very rare that two people having sex for the first time will know each other's ins and outs. It's foolish to assume that someone will know how you like it, where you like it, when, and why. Even though you may believe you've descended from Aphrodite herself, and that Eros, Homers, and Pothos take sex advice from you, it doesn't mean you'll be able to produce a sexual masterpiece in the bedroom with your new lover. Why? Because as much as we'd like to think sex is all a physical act, the truth is much different.

Sure, anyone and everyone can get themselves off, but to truly create that sexual experience for another that rearranges the body, seduces the mind, and rebirths the soul, you need more experience . . . with that person. You need the kind of experience that involves progressing out of the Bust-Down Worthy stage. Ideally, you'd want to wait until you guys have progressed to truly D8able status, but because that could take a while, realistically you two will probably give in to sexual temptation somewhere in the Friendship stage. Put it this way: the more you know, the better chance you have to truly create an amazing experience in the bedroom.

The other huge fallacy is the belief that sex will keep somebody, or make them act the way you want them to. Newsflash: sex isn't a secret weapon, no matter how many times those shitty corner-store magazines tell you it is. Someone may act a certain way to get to the sex, but sex alone isn't going to keep them there. Drop the princess complex and the manufactured prince charming ideas. Your vagina isn't the exclusive platinum model and your dick doesn't cure cancer. If all you have to offer is sex, then you're no different from the next guy with perfect hair, and an expensive French scent, trying to balance on a barstool without spilling his scotch.

Think about it for a minute. Did any of your expedited sex partners stick around? Probably not. Now look at the more successful relationships you've had over the course of your dating career. What do you have there? The time it took to hop in the sack probably varied from relationship to relationship. Your previous love interests probably didn't look exactly alike. The one common denominator that your more successful relationships had was that you and your previous partners actually connected on different levels other than the physical.

For those of you who haven't had successful relationships quite yet, ask yourselves what was missing? Did you guys know enough about each other? Was he a lying, cheating canine? Were you a lying, cheating, sex-crazed animal? Whatever the reason associated with your respective failed unions, you can probably associate it with lack of information. You didn't have enough evidence that he was a fuck-boy. You guys didn't spend enough time learning about each other, so the sex was wack as well as the rest of the relationship. Something was missing and you didn't have enough mutual insight to pick up on it. So, holding back the goods for a while is more so to allow time to learn about each other than it is about seeming less like a ho or playing hard to get.

Because the first interaction with a potential love interest is clearly on the physical level, and because you don't know anything about them initially, it makes sense that sex with them would be one of the first things you think of. That does not mean, however, that sex needs to be the first step in creating a relationship. If you guys have that explosive physical chemistry, guess what? It's not going anywhere. For the most part, three months from now he'll still be hot, and he'll still want to get you naked. Furthermore, he'll still consider you a hottie as well, and you'll definitely still want to get him naked. As a matter of fact, the want will probably be amplified because of the waiting process. That, along with actually getting to know someone, and liking what you find out, can fortify whatever sexual chemistry you thought you had when you two knew nothing of each other.

Imagine how much of an ego stroke it would be to know how to mentally stimulate the guy before you've even seen him with his shirt off. Think of the confidence and sexiness you'd exude walking into that bedroom for the first time. Now imagine how well all of this would be reciprocated by someone who actually took the time to find out how to activate those pleasure centers in your brain.

File their hotness away in your mental database and try to focus on other things, because the sex isn't going anywhere. It does, however, stand the chance to improve even before you know what you're improving on. It sounds cliché as hell, but time really does reveal all, either through realization or education.

Game On

The dating world is a lot like ancient mythology. There are quite a bit of hidden truths buried amongst a sea of fanatical story, hearsay, and downright lies. This sea of nonsensical intelligence has developed over the years and its tide has continued to rise. The trick is to filter out the impurities in hopes of getting the freshest, purest understanding of where you sit in this chess game called relationships, and learning the best moves to make in these specific time frames.

Yes, dating and relationships are a lot like chess. The other person makes a move, you counter. You're trying to think three moves ahead;

if they do this, I'll do that. Their defenses are up, protecting their heart at all costs. Your defenses are up; you've dealt with too many assholes before. You're trying to break the other person's defenses down while guarding your own. All the while, they're trying to get you in check position. The true winners, of course, are the two people who reach a stalemate because both realize that they're evenly matched. Somewhere during the history of dating, however, bullshit defenses and downright stupid offensive maneuvers were introduced into the game by mentally novice players . . . The problem is, a lot of that dysfunctional folly still exists within the game.

Certain things are just silly. The whole "not calling someone for three days" methodology comes to mind. Why does it matter if you call them the following day if you two hit it off today? The reasoning behind this is because you don't want to seem so accessible, so needy so early in the game. There are a million and one ways to be an instant stalker than calling someone the next day. Not to mention, if you really are the clingy type, your Velcro personality is going to come out at some point. Faking the funk now isn't going to protect you later. That clingy shit is something you need to get a hold on before you start dating anyway (to be discussed later).

There are more little stupid diversions and mental obstacles we use in the belief that they'll help us either catch someone or keep them. Many more, more than we can count. We do dumb shit, like purposely doing things to make a potential significant other jealous. Does he really need to know about *every* person who hits on you? We impose tests to see how much we mean to the other person . . . C'mon, you know you've done it. The all-time worst is presenting ultimatums with you on one side and something your love interest holds dear on the other. "Janet, if you really loved me you'd give up writing and get a more stable office job and be with me." No, Janet needs to love herself and leave you standing there with your silly games, child's play, and a sex toy to keep you company. That type of soul-abusing activity should be punishable in a court of law.

Some of the things we think are positioning us to create a relationship or strengthen an existing union actually help to unravel the fabric of what we're trying to build. So the next time a friend tells you it's okay to flaunt would-be suitors in front of the guy you're dating, do yourself a favor and block that friend. Think clearly and evaluate if the course of action you're taking is actually detrimental to you progressing through a relationship with someone.

The chess moves you make should be, first and foremost, focusing on fortifying yourself in the dating game. Secondly, the moves you make should be actively strengthening your chance to develop something real with your potential significant other. If at any time your moves feel somewhat manipulative, they probably are. If your actions seem a lot like kids' games, they probably are. As always, because every scenario has two sides, be mindful of the strategies your potential significant other chooses to utilize as well. Are they grown-up chess moves, or silly Chutes and Ladders plays? Go for the grown-up moves.

One . . . Two . . . Three . . . Four . . . Five

The importance of the Three-Date Rule, or the Ten-Date Rule, or the Three-Month Rule, or the "No Sex before Monogamy" Rule is what they represent more than any time frame referenced. When the no-sex-before-monogamy ideology first arose, it's doubtful that the originators (whoever they may be) really knew what they were on to. "Make him wait. If he's still around, then it means he really likes you." But why is that? Why were people so convinced that making someone wait was the way to go? Was it the belief that playing hard to get was the route to take to coax the affections out of a suitor? Maybe secretly the ideology behind the waiting was similar to the effects of someone finding an oasis in the desert: they've waited so long that any action they get is going to feel like the best action they've ever had, which will in turn make them want to stay . . .

Whatever the reason, the waiting motif has stood the test of time

Whether it was realized or not, the emphasis of these respective guidelines is on promoting an environment conducive to getting the two parties actively involved in learning about each other on a deeper level other than just the physical, sexual plane. These guidelines represent a very proactive and healthy approach to dating. This is because the person abiding by these guidelines is deliberately attempting to sculpt their relationship as they see fit. They're not running into a relationship blind with their pants down, hoping for the best. They're systematically trying to protect themselves, while at the same time absorbing as much information as possible from a potential mate.

Enter the D8able Five-Date Rule

Our Five-Date Rule is designed to be used as a blueprint to kind of take you through what your first five major meet-ups with your potential mate represent. More than simply rendezvous, the dates described represent different comfort levels reached while dating someone on the way to the end goal of being comfortable enough with the relationship to sleep with your potential mate. Now, it's no guarantee that after five dates you two will be ready to sleep together, but you'll be a hell of lot better off than running into a bar with a blindfold on, swinging your dick around, hoping for a match.

The Interview

The first date. Yes, the first date is, in essence, an interview. The first time you make someone's acquaintance, say, at a bar or your local car wash, is the equivalent of you turning on your laptop, polishing up your resume, and submitting it for a job online. The first date is in fact the equivalent of an interview because the two of you are feeling each other out to see if you might fit well together. Good first dates aren't necessarily elaborate, expensive excursions. They definitely aren't activities that promote minimal interaction between the two of you. Much like an interview for a new position, good first dates are opportunities to share heavier, detailed information about each other.

Remember how we all transition through the phases, and the mini plateaus within the stages? Well, the first date is the direct effect of each of you realizing that the other has the potential to be more than one in a pool of Bust-Down Worthy folks. Maybe you've spent a ton of time texting or talking. Maybe that first meeting was so powerful that you both propelled out of the first stage and into the Friendship phase. Whatever the reason, you two have made enough of a positive impact on each other to where imagining each other naked is only the icing on a potentially much more substantial cake. Whereas the Superficial Spark is much more of a random—or as some may call it, lucky—occurrence (even swiping through dating profiles, though deliberate, has an element of luck involved), the first date is deliberate. It represents the two of you intentionally taking steps to assess the development of an intimate relationship.

The first date is the realization that your potential other half has enough going on for you to initiate their journey through the Friendship phase. This is an important development socially as well. You're admitting to yourself that the person you once considered only as a sexual diversion could very well develop into a much more substantial character in a life story starring you. As a matter of fact, the first date is you actively entertaining the idea that this person could take you off the market, which is a scary notion for the nice guys and player-types alike. Because of this, a bit of care should be taken in choosing the setting for a first date.

There are no right answers in developing a first-date scenario, but there are a lot of wrong choices. Does that make sense? The first date needs to promote as much interaction between the two of you as possible. It should also stray away from the boring clichés. Dinner and a movie is cool on a lazy Sunday, when you two have been together for six or seven years. It should not, however, even be an option, a thought, or a flicker between the synapses in the thinking areas of the brain for the first date. Why? First of all, dinner and a movie is the cliché of clichés.

When you think of the most mundane, routine excursion you can engage in, dinner and a movie is at the top of the list. It's boring as hell, and it shows that you really didn't put any thought into the first meeting. It's right up there with grabbing a cup of coffee, which is probably more of a beneficial first meeting because at least you can converse and learn a few things about each other. If you can recall some of the first dates you've had, which ones were the more enjoyable ones? Which first dates didn't turn out so well? A wager could be made that the more enjoyable dates you've had, especially first-date scenarios, were the ones that didn't seem like routine meetings.

Scenarios like dinner and a movie, or going to a play, or even going to a concert aren't a good idea for a first date. This is because you guys will spend the majority of the date paying attention to the third party instead of each other. Your ability to learn about each other will be severely impaired because of the outside distraction. You can't have a conversation about anything substantial if you're busy watching Denzel Washington on screen. You can't hear each other, and therefore you can't learn about one another, when Beyoncé is harmonizing into a microphone. And it's just uncouth to talk during a play.

Most importantly, you need to remember what the first date is about. To a lesser extent, first dates help with initially determining the placement of your potential love interest in the Friendship phase. Will they be closer to D8able status after your first meeting, or will they be knocked down a few stairs? Ultimately, however, it's about finding commonalities and interesting differences about each other that'll set the groundwork to continue dating. Because of this, you want to set a scene that will give you two the best shot at really connecting. Minimizing outside distraction is key. Fostering an environment for wrapping your minds around each other is imperative. You don't want a bad first date to prematurely end something with the potential to be great.

How many crappy first dates have you been on that led to second encounters?

It's probably better to lean toward a meeting that's heavy on conversation and physical interaction. The first date, if you're planning it, should also have elements in it that you know your potential mate would enjoy. These are things, of course, that you would learn through the course of conversation long before the date. It'll make a good impression, as well as lighten the mood, because you'll be participating in an activity you're both comfortable with. The quicker you can get past the initial awkwardness of a first meeting, the quicker you can get to the all-important rapport building, or deconstructing, whatever the case may be.

By the end of your first date, you should have a better grasp of exactly whom this person is, just as they should have a better understanding of who you are as well. If the date goes well enough, a second date is definitely in order. If the date sucked royally, your dating initiate may either stall out at their Friendship mini plateau or fall down a few pegs. Worst-case scenario, they could very well plummet through the Bust-Down Worthy stage and end up as a nobody, not even a blip on your dating radar. But hey, that's what dating is for, to weed out the nobodies. Not everyone attains the job they apply for.

Ante Up

Date numero dos. Welcome to the higher-stakes round. You've gotten the nervousness caused by the initial date out of your system at this point. You two have clearly been communicating since then. Rapport is clearly continuing to develop. Date number two should be all about fun, with information gathering sprinkled in. Well, you're always learning about your potential mate, but because you've pretty much cemented a mutual "like" between the two of you, date number two can predominantly be focused on enjoying a real-world activity together. Of course, the real-world activity is based on your respective preferences.

Just because everything went well on your first date doesn't mean you should downplay the importance of your second meeting. The stars could've been aligned. Your first date may have been a very favorable fluke. The second date can be used as a gauge to see if the feelings birthed during the first meeting will reach adolescence during your second date.

The second date can also be considered a pillar of some sort. If date number one was all about getting to know someone in real time, then date number two usually encompasses learning more about your potential mate's passions and the things they find enjoyable. This is not to say that excellent date rapport can't be reached on the first date, but as stated earlier, the first date really serves to see if you guys have what it takes to date. Date number two and its subsequent meet-ups tend to focus more on how you guys interact together in the real world.

Think about it for a second. When you head out on a second date, what is the foundation of this particular meeting? Date number two usually focuses on some sort of activity the two of you both like to do or are familiar with. More often than not, it's an activity that most people enjoy. The excursion could be something as simple as shooting pool. Though you've reached a certain level of comfort with your dating initiate, it is not out of the ordinary to choose a generally enjoyable experience as a sort of safety net. Whether or not it's done purposely, this setup is probably your best bet for two reasons: Firstly, it eliminates the anxiety of choosing an outing that may not sit favorably with your date. Secondly, it allows you two to continue to build rapport, but on a different level.

Your first meeting was about finding certain commonalities and interesting differences in a general sense. The second date is an exploration of things mutually enjoyable. The environment should be conducive to being more playful with each other. You guys are more relaxed, so it's less like an interview and more like two friends having a good time together.

And that's exactly as it should be . . . two friends enjoying each other's company.

It probably doesn't need to be said how important it is to enjoy each other's company. Having things in common with someone is very important, but if you don't enjoy being around that person, then it doesn't make much of a difference, does it? This is why date number two is so important. It can be the encounter that reveals how well you two get along. It can be the make-or-break situation. If all goes well, dates three and beyond have a solid chance of taking place. If not, you may find yourselves relocated to a lower tier of the Friendship phase, if not eliminated completely (depending on how badly the date goes).

Hump Date

Welcome to the third installment of "Your Fledgling Dating Life." You are, of course, the star of this tale. As it stands, you've met someone who seems to have great potential to be that special one. You clicked on date one, and date two was like a reunion of old flames. What's left? Icing the cake, of course.

By the time you guys have reached date three, you should have enough information and a strong enough rapport that the planner (let's assume it's you) can create a real, lasting impression of a date. This is your time to really shine. Creating an experience rooted in things your date finds specifically enjoyable is the route to take on this adventure. It'll accomplish quite a bit in fortifying the brand-new union you're constructing. This will be your love interest's first real exposure to how attentive of a mate you can be.

Sure, anyone can reread a string of texts and regurgitate someone's likes and dislikes, someone's food preferences, or someone's favorite vacation spots. Going out of your way to honor those particular preferences is another thing entirely. People love it when the person they're dating can show that even the smallest detail hasn't escaped unnoticed. Actions such as these go a long way in conveying how important someone is to their mate. If they're into you the way you're into them, an act such as this will really resonate with them. Dating is a chess game and you've made a major move to position yourself for the check.

Just remember, the smart dater realizes that the actions taken to catch someone are not the deeds you need to do to keep them—nor should you downgrade said actions after nabbing your love interest. They are in fact a foundation upon which to build. Every good deed, every sympathetic and caring act, is a brick added to the relationship structure you're creating.

The Cement

Your fourth date is more of the same. If you've made it this far, then it's pretty much understood between you two that you're in fact dating. The fourth date is a representation of how you two should strive to treat each other during the course of your relationship. If the third date is your foundation, your fourth date and beyond embody the relationship you build over the foundation as you both work toward transitioning from the Friendship phase through the D8able phase.

In an ideal scenario, the fourth date, after you've waited and learned about your new mate, is the time frame when you're ready to take your physical intimacy to the next level. You both have proved to each other that you care about one another on a higher level other than just sex. You've dated. You've connected mentally. You've explored your common interests, and you respect and are attracted to your respective differences. You've even begun, to some extent, to find new adventures to enjoy together.

Even if it hasn't been formally discussed, for all intents and purposes, you two are an item.

The caring that you show to your new love interest should naturally be returned to you. Furthermore, you should feel relatively comfortable and secure with the idea of the two of you as a unit. It's been said before, but there is no harm in mentioning it again: relationships are always a two-way street. It is not the case that you should engage in loving activity only for the sake of gaining it in return. No, you do things for the person you're dating because you genuinely care about them. They need to do the same for you as well, and for the same reasons, because they genuinely care. They should not be giving you the bare minimum for pacification purposes just to keep you around. They should be proactively showing you that you mean as much to them as they mean to you. This is not to say that you should quantify what your soon-to-be significant other does for you, but you should feel that sense of home—that sense of security—with them. You should truly believe that the person you want to be your other half cares for you as they would naturally care for themselves.

Remember that people display the way they care in different ways. Your potential other half may not express certain things the way you do. It doesn't mean that they don't care, it just means that their affinity for you may manifest differently from your displays of affection for them. You should still be able to think clearly and realize whether or not this person has your best interests at heart. The true sign that you're ready to transition to a higher form of relationship is when your heart and mind can sit at the same table and agree on this issue . . . that in fact, this person cares about you.

Monogamy and Sex

You've reached the finish line. The fifth date. Your brain, your heart, and your reproductive equipment all point, literally and figuratively, to one person in particular. Though it doesn't necessarily have to be stated, you both should definitely be on the same page. The sex time is a game between two people, and only two people. You two people. You don't want any surprise guest stars showing up on set, nor does your new significant other want to find out that someone else is auditioning for the role.

Once that understanding has been clearly reached, you can safely do what grown folks do.

Up to this point, you guys have been exploring each other on a deeper level. You should feel like the person in front of you knows you for who you really are. They should feel the same about you. The physical attraction created the gravitational pull between you two. The mental attraction and connection will hold you together. Because saints don't exist anymore, you two have probably come close to breaking that "no sex until monogamy" rule, which isn't a bad thing. We're human and we all have needs, including those of a physical nature. The intimate play-and-stop sessions do an excellent job in building that want. Coupled with the rapport building you've been doing on a more cerebral level, you two have been creating a rather powerful bond.

You see, relationships aren't rocket science. Certain magazines would have you believe they are because they want to sell subscriptions. "Fifteen Ways to Please Your Man" is bullshit. The strength of a relationship comes from building a rapport on three levels with your mate: the physical affinity and admiration, plus the mental connection and appreciation, plus the ability to put the other person's needs before your own (which can be considered a rather spiritual link) equal a bad-ass, airtight union.

The real reason why no sex before monogamy is preached here in this text is not to exact a childlike game of hide-and-seek. It's not even about holding out to make the other person work, even if it does happen to be an Ivy League course load at times. No sex before monogamy is promoted here to protect you from would-be predators, yes, but more importantly it is promoted to protect you from yourself. It gives you the opportunity to learn about yourself with this other person. You also learn how your love interest interacts with you. It protects your higher form of thinking from being clouded by your little head and its superficial brain. You're creating a stronger foundation built upon knowing yourself as a complete person in a relationship, as well as on understanding and caring for another complete person. The realization and compartmentalization of your superficiality, so it doesn't run rampant, are the only ways you'll have a shot at truly learning these things. Once you can get your brain and your heart and your dick working on the same page, you are a much more fortified person in the dating game.

Dating Mistakes We All Make

Humans are emotional creatures, as you very well know at this point. We are also very reactionary, which you're also very much aware of. Because of this, even the most seasoned dater can end up taking the wrong route while playing the dating game. We want certain things on an emotional and physical level, especially when dealing with someone we like. We have also been taught to play the game, in our own way, to get what we want. The problem is, certain courses of action can actually stunt what you're trying to accomplish in the dating game.

We tend to seek counsel from people who have no business giving it, simply because they're friends and trusted folks. When we're in a bind, especially a bind involving the heart, we seek help from these people. How many times has your single, no-man-having, bitter-ass friend freely given up "foolproof" advice on dating? If it's so foolproof, then why is your know-it-all friend still swiping right on a random dating app? If you can't recall a recent time that this friend has accomplished anything successful in the dating world, you may want to slide this very manual to them, because they damn sure aren't qualified to be helping others.

Self-Objectification and Seduction

Another boneheaded move people tend to make, especially in the social media age, is mistaking self-objectification for seduction. You've either seen it or done it, or know someone that's done it. Seduction, true seduction, does not involve sending naked photos, dick pics, or ass shots to someone you barely know. Remember that superficial brain that keeps getting mentioned? Well, sending forty-seven dick pics to a random person you met three days ago isn't going to motivate them to know you on a deeper level. It will, however, feed that superficial, objectifying portion of their brain, causing you to be placed squarely in the Bust-Down Worthy phase. You're openly telling this random person that it's okay to objectify you, because you're readily objectifying yourself for a little bit of attention.

And what sort of attention is it? Not the kind that leads to the deep emotional understanding needed for a relationship, which was described earlier.

Not leaving anything to the imagination is not a functional form of seduction either. There is a huge difference in being verbally alluring and just sounding like a streetwalker on the stroll trying to pick up a paying John. Does the brand-new interest really need to know how, when, and where you can milk their love juices out of them . . . the second time you speak? It makes you look desperate, which is definitely a one-way ticket to One-Night Standville, in the state of Bust Down. Just don't do it. Show some respect for yourself in order to get respect from others.

That Thirsty Feeling

When we admit to ourselves that we really like someone, our common sense can take a backseat to a hunger for acceptance by that person. Being too available too soon is a common mistake and common form of emotional indentured servitude that many of us willfully enter into. Remember, dating is a learning process, on both sides. They're learning about you, and you them. Just because the surface of your new, shiny love interest is awesome doesn't mean the core is pristine. Going too far out of your way for someone who hasn't proven:

A. That they like you in the same way or
B. That they deserve said treatment

Just puts you in a predicament. You're either setting yourself up to be used or setting yourself up to be left behind, because you'll appear to be desperate for affection once again. Now, don't get it wrong. It's great to want to be there for someone, to have their back during hard times, to be every hallmark card ever with your love interest. But, take a step back and look at your situation. Is this person worthy of the royal treatment? Meaning, are they treating you the same way? If your situation seems one-sided, it probably is.

Cold as Ice?

On the flip side, many folks try to make themselves too unavailable in an attempt to play out a childish game of cat-and-mouse. Well, if you know anything about cats, they don't bother with things that are too easy to catch or too hard. You need to have a healthy balance. Acting too busy or too important to be bothered with someone you like is one of the most effective ways to not have that person around anymore. It's better to be up front, to be yourself, than it would ever be to play any extreme.

The Fuck-Buddy Problem

Fuck buddies are another dating snafu. Sexual playmates are fun when you're open and single. We've all had them. Some of you probably have two or three as you read this. Having a fuck-buddy while you're seriously trying to get to know someone else is just not a good idea. We love to think we can compartmentalize emotion. "I won't possibly catch feelings for Tim, it's just sex." Bullshit. There is always a level of feeling exchanged for all intimate situations regardless of whether or not you think so. Having that third party around keeps you from being able to focus on the potential mate. Physical connection is a part of connecting with someone. If you have that connection with Tim while you're trying to learn about Kevin, Kevin's not going to get the full you experience. Plus, you'll have that fuck-buddy as a crutch. You'll be spreading yourself emotionally thin like the last piece of butter on Texas Toast. Worst-case scenario, you try to cut the playmate off to move forward with your new love and the playmate doesn't go into the dark quietly. It is not out of the realm of possibility that fuck-buddy becomes fuck-boy and tries to hate on your new interest. It is in your best interest to distance yourself from the substitute freak once you realize you want to get to know the new person.

Playing with Players

One of the most glaring deficiencies people tend to have is the uncanny lack of ability to differentiate between players and genuine people. Emotion and initial infatuation can cloud your mind when it comes to spotting these guys. Give the players credit, they can be amazingly effective at what they do. Silver tongues and smooth moves can leave many people feeling lost and turned out. Fortifying the mental side of your being is the only way to separate the snakes from the grass.

It was mentioned previously, but players operate on their own timetable. This is a huge red flag. If you feel as though you're being pushed in a direction that you're not very comfortable with, you could be dealing with the player-type. If you feel as if you're operating on their timetable, you could be dealing with a player, or at the least a jerk who's unwilling to compromise. You see, at their core is a self-ish person trying to get something out of you. You need to look past the smooth language and sexual attraction. Base your relationship's state on actions and actions alone. A person who respects you, and this includes emotionally, will not press you to do things you aren't comfortable with. Someone who's truly into you would want you to be comfortable with the progression of your relationship because they value how you feel, even more than they value their own feelings. Be observant; all things are revealed in time . . . Hence, the Five-Date Methodology.

Look out for pacification as well. The simplest explanation for this is taking bare minimum action to keep you around. Once a player gets what they want, or even before they do, if they keep you around, their actions become very evident. They go from being very proactive to very reactive. They don't work ahead of time to keep you happy, they work after the fact to put out any emotional fires. They aren't trying to move the relationship forward; they're trying to keep it right where it is. Now, don't go jumping into the deep end. Some of us can be super demanding and hard to please. So take a look at yourself and your demanding ways before you go labeling everybody a player. It could be that you need to turn your inner diva's volume down a bit.

CHAPTER 3

80/20

PERIODIC TABLE IN FULL

Do you believe in such a thing as that 100 percent perfect relationship? Not even the creators of children's fairy tales could properly illustrate the idea of a flawless union, which is why we never find out about prince charming and the damsel after he's returned her mystical footwear, or acted as her alarm clock, or rescued her from some ridiculously constructed tower. Not even the most optimistic, imaginative human brain can fathom a blemish-free relationship, because it doesn't exist. Period.

The idea of the perfect relationship is the twin brother to your laundry list for the perfect mate. Both are conceived in the same place and are the product of your heart getting your head high off rainbows, snorting puppies, and shooting red roses into your brain. As much as we'd like to believe in the existence of a single soul mate, and the possibility of relationship perfection, we tend to forget one very important component of all this: ourselves. Simply put, there is no such thing as the perfect relationship, because we aren't perfect.

As human beings, we have shortcomings. We make mistakes. We have the negative aspects of our respective makeups along with the good qualities. We are flawed; therefore, we cannot expect any relationship we're a part of to be perfect. But, just because a relationship isn't perfect doesn't mean it can't work perfectly for you. And, just because your potential mate isn't perfect doesn't mean they can't be perfect for you. On the flip side, your perfect set of imperfections could be exactly what someone else may need.

If you can admit to yourself that nothing and no one is perfect . . .

B Average

The 80/20 rule was made popular by a certain Tyler Perry movie, *Why Did I Get Married?* Though nothing is as cut-and-dry as a principle such as this, we can learn a lot from what it stands for. The 80/20 principle essentially teaches that no one, including us, is perfect. Because of this, any relationship we'll be a part of will not be perfect either. This principle helps to give you a more realistic sense of the way relationships work.

This principle teaches that because we're imperfect beings, when it comes to relationships, we can expect only to receive 80 percent of what we want in a relationship from our mate. That other 20 percent stands for the things we may not see too often or may never see from our love interests. The actual figures aren't important here. There's no possible way to actually quantify what you do and do not receive from your significant other.

What you're supposed to take away from the principle is the idea that, when you're in a relationship with a good person, you'll receive far more than what you'll be missing out on. For instance, the guy you're with may treat you like royalty. He may wine, dine, and take you on adventures. He'll genuinely show that he loves and cares for you. The only drawback is that maybe his abs don't look the way you'd like them to, or maybe you guys don't share the same interest in certain extracurricular activities.

When you read the examples here, the negatives seem trivial in comparison to how great the guy actually is. The 80/20 principle, without spelling it out for you, is yet another tool to be used to get you to break your previous cycle of shallow thinking when it comes to dating and relationships, as well as overall matters of the heart.

If you look at the principle for what it is, you'll understand that the 80/20 rule is the anti-laundry list. It is the superficial-mentality suppressant. It is an ideology that fully challenges any fairy tale's attempt to drown us in the indication that a superhero love interest exists, and that this love interest is waiting somewhere in the sky to swoop down and somehow save us from the imperfect relationship. Lastly and most importantly, the 80/20 rule, just like the rest of the ideas in this manual, forces you to look at just how much you bring to the table in a relationship.

The 80/20 principle also forces you to accept people for who they are. It teaches compromise because you can't, in fact, have a 100 percent relationship, just as you can't have the perfect mate. You guys will never see eye to eye on everything, and you don't have to. The 80/20 rule helps you to shed the fairy tale 3-D glasses for a look at the real world. Only babies think they can have everything they want, right when they want it. Adults need to learn to compromise, especially in intimate relationships.

Though it doesn't imply this, the 80/20 rule should be a reminder that you should strive to cover that so-called 20 percent you don't have. Relationships are and will forever be work. You have to work to keep it alive. You have to work to keep your relationship enjoyable. You have to work to make sure that the feelings and emotions involved in the creation of said relationship endure, and even grow. You need to focus on that "80 percent" you do have, and make it the best "80 percent" possible. A relationship is no place for an emotionally lazy person.

Complacency can be, and usually is, the death of a relationship. Don't allow yourself to get too comfortable. Don't forget what you did to catch your mate. Strive to keep your relationship flying in the right direction. The things you did to get your mate should be the foundation to erect a skyscraper-like union. They should not be the standard.

Also, do not drown in what's missing. You may wake up one day and realize that your relationship dried out because you wasted all your time wearing water wings, wading in a puddle of have-nots instead of diving into the deep end and enjoying all the beauty you two brought to the union. Improvement and progress have never been born out of wallowing in negativity. Instead, identify your deficiencies and use them as the fuel to develop what you bring to the relationship.

The Relative 80 Percent

As with everything else in dating and relationships, certain elements of the 80/20 rule are foundational and should be on everyone's list. Other things are totally up to the preference of the individual. For instance, a part of the 80 percent that all mates should possess, at the least, is the need to respect their significant other. This shouldn't be a want, but an imperative. If you're dealing with someone who's only respectful when it's convenient for them, then their ratio of existent to nonexistent qualities is totally off and should be up for a strict evaluation by you. Other things, like a sense of adventure or an enjoyment of cooking, are based on preference.

In the grand scheme of things, first and foremost you should make sure all of the universally sought-after traits exist in your mate. After you know this person really cares for you, then you can worry about the other qualities they may or may not possess.

All personality traits are not created equally, as we discussed in previous chapters. Please reread if you're not familiar with the idea. There is the possibility that a particular character trait you really need finds its way into the 20 percent portion. If this is the case, then you may really need to evaluate whether or not the other 80 percent is something worth preserving. But, typically, the 20 percent that may be missing from your relationship is similar to the difference between a regular-sized order of fries and a super-sized order. Sure you'd like the extra french fries, but you don't need them to have a fulfilling meal.

Don't lie to yourself about the 80 percent your mate possesses. If you feel like you're truly missing something substantial, go back a few chapters and review how to categorize the different qualities your love interest has. Honest evaluation will help to determine if your significant other has the key elements necessary to give you a relatively fulfilled intimate experience. If, for example, you evaluate your relationship and come to find out that your mate is perfect, but they're actually a cheater . . . then you know you're not in the right scenario. Be honest with yourself either way.

Drowning in the Kiddie Pool

This is what focusing on the 20 percent is. Here you are submersed in the anger and doubt that inevitably floods an insecure relationship, all because of the stupid 20 percent you perceive to be missing. Guess what? It's your own damn fault. It was you who flung the blades of doubt into your relationship, poking holes in your union. It was you who opened the windows during a drizzle, allowed everything to get wet, and mistook it for a storm. If you would take a second, plant your feet, and think clearly, you could easily stand up in your relationship and realize you were face-first in a shallow pool of relationship stupidity. If this sounds harsh, then good. It's meant to.

Do you know what complaining about a perceived lack of 20 percent in a relationship is like? Imagine a rich man with a vault full of money. The only thing is, he needs to guard that vault because there are no locks on the doors. This man spots a roll of quarters down the street from the vault. He endlessly obsesses over how much more rich he could be if only he had that $10 worth of coins . . .

Day and night he tries to figure out how to get that money. He believes that the $10 will somehow bring him the happiness he lacks with the other $100 million he has in his vault. He fixates on the quarters, all the while not noticing the thieves sneaking into his vault, pocketing his real treasure. By the time he realizes what's going on, he's damn near broke because of a stack of quarters that weren't even worth his time.

The misguided fixation on the little you don't have introduces negativity into your relationship that threatens to destroy all that you do have. Once again, it must be said that relationships are in fact a two-way street. It is not necessarily the case that you'll be the one to walk away over that missing nominal percentage. Your loved one could very well be the person who gets fed up with you because of your infantile frustration in the matter.

Some people are aware of their misguided focus. Others don't have a clue. Maybe it's because we're taught to strive for perfection in all things. Maybe it's the delusional belief that we are somehow perfect and therefore deserve perfection (princess complex). Whatever the origin of our misguided fixation, if the dysfunctional focus is left unchecked, you stand the chance of having to reread this manual because you'll be starting all over again.

Observe the Negative

Regardless of why, we'd all probably agree that people are geared to focus on the negative. We're almost drawn to the negative aspects of our lives and other people's lives like flies to dog shit. Just take a look at society as a whole. Bad car crashes create gapers' delays. Something in us compels us to sit there and watch the mess of a car sandwich. Fights are another example. We can't get enough of conflict—the bloodier the better. We'll pause the movie we're watching on Netflix if it means hearing a neighbor's argument more clearly.

A whole chapter could be written on reality TV. The uplifting, positive shows last about a week. The programs that showcase the epitome of human ignorance, the fighting, the lunacy, the airing of every piece of soiled unmentionables, last for years. When one finally does expire, a new shit-slinging reality show takes its place. And the news . . . Where could we start with the news? When's the last time you heard an inspiring, heartwarming story on your local news channel? It doesn't happen too often. But, you're pretty much guaranteed to be exposed to adverse issues affecting your area.

You know those beloved corner-store magazines you can't wait to buy every month? Most of these things are better used as colorful toilet paper. The self-esteem-damaging malarkey in some of these glossy pieces of butt by-product can be astounding. The writers spend the majority of their time describing to their readers exactly why the reader isn't good enough, without offering any real solutions. The bullshit they mask as a solution is nothing more than a ploy to trick you into buying stuff you don't need. They sell you lip-serviced emotional bandages for wounds that don't even exist. Just take a look at some of the articles. Most of the dating advice given never even mentions the importance of self-appreciation and development. But, you can bet an article or seven hundred exists about the utilization of some superficial tactic to attract someone. Funny, none of them even suggest (or give any substantial information on) how to maintain and cultivate relationships through self-maintenance and personal growth. Some of them even play up the perceived 20 percent you may be missing in your relationship. "Wear this dress, it'll make you look slimmer." "This star does this, you should too." "Ten ways to please your mate . . ." Useless nonsense.

Some of your friends and family, though they mean well, give the dumbest advice ever in regard to dating and relationships. And why is it always your eternally single buddy who always claims to know how to catch, stroke, and keep a significant other? We're human, and from time to time, we all need a sounding board. But, discussion of relationship issues with a third party not directly involved in the relationship may not be the best idea, especially when they can't give you an objective opinion. It's bad enough that some of us focus on the 20 percent missing from the relationship. The last thing you need is to have somebody ignorant of the relationship helping you focus on that negative 20 percent, but a lot of people do.

With all of this negative reinforcement around us, it's no wonder that so many of us focus on what we don't have, instead of on the positive pieces in our respective lives. This includes our dating lives.

20 Percent

Why is the 20 percent we're not getting so damned alluring at times? The answer is simple enough, and it mirrors a sentiment we discussed earlier. We want what we can't have. If you can remember, a few chapters back, we discussed relationship "types." And even before that we discussed the superficially rooted laundry list of potential-mate characteristics. All three of these thought processes are tied into the idealistic center of the brain.

We want the perfect mate. We want whom we perceive to be our type, and we want our type to fit perfectly with us in our respective fairy tale relationships. The very place that initiates attraction, and therefore is the catalyst for relationships to begin, is also the same place where our unrealistic views and requirements for relationships are born. Coincidentally this is also the very same place that would have us believe we can have a 100 percent relationship. Remember, we believe we can achieve perfection in all things. Not to mention that the chase for perfection is one of those things that is instilled in us as children. When did your parents ever tell you to strive for an 80 percent on a test? Probably never.

This is what makes the missing 20 percent so powerful . . . We're taught to chase perfection in all things. We're taught to ignore our flaws. We don't take into account that our own imperfections make it virtually impossible to live in a flawless union with another flawed being. All of this is what makes the unattainable so appealing.

It can also trick the superficially foggy-brained dater into believing that the 20 percent they don't have is somehow better than the 80 percent they do possess . . .

Before you read any farther, you need to understand this concrete law of dating and relationships. You cannot build a better mate. In the history of dating, this has never happened successfully. Trying to fix a mate in an attempt to produce that missing 20 percent is probably one of the more futile efforts you can ever attempt. No one, repeat, no one, has ever changed because someone else wanted that person to. They change only when they're good and ready to make that change. No amount of coercion, nagging, or any other tactic can change this. You need to go into the relationship accepting the person for who they are from the get-go. You need to have the mind-set that this is who they are and they probably won't change. If you can accept that, then you'll be better off and the 80/20 rule will be much more helpful to you. Don't go in thinking you've got yourself a fixer-upper mate. People are not possessions that can be modified at the whim of another.

As stated before, focusing your energies in the wrong direction will almost certainly lead to the unraveling of your relationship. The healthy 80 percent that you have needs to be cared for above all else. While communication is key and the backbone of any relationship, and when used correctly can help to improve the lacking 20 percent, you can't allow that healthy 80 percent to wither while trying to manufacture the missing 20 percent. Your best bet is to spend about 80 percent of your time fostering what works, while attempting to develop stronger bonds to improve the weak 20 percent. But, by no means should you risk your sure-thing 80 percent in an attempt to corral the missing 20 percent at home or away.

What Would You Do For . . .

That other 20 percent? Would you cheat? People do, all the time. You can read editorials on the topic of cheating. You can even read scientific journals on the subject. Most of these pieces come to the same conclusion. People usually cheat because they feel like their relationships are missing something. Man or woman, it's all the same. On the surface, it may appear as if the motivations are different, but the root cause is the same: there's something missing.

Sure, the excitement of getting something you previously didn't have is very powerful. Everyone remembers a Christmas when Santa hooked you up with the exact present you wanted. You were on cloud nine until January 2. You also forgot about all the other gifts you had received. For that brief moment in time, the gift you had just opened was the coolest thing on the face of planet Earth.

This is in essence what it feels like to cheat, especially if attaining that missing 20 percent is the motivation for your infidelity. Finally, getting that 20 percent feels pretty fucking amazing, but just like last year's Christmas gift, cheating will not make up for all the other things you receive in a good relationship with a good mate. There is no guarantee that the 20 percent you're receiving now will even last. There's also no guarantee that the person you're getting that new, shiny 20 percent from is even capable of giving you the 80 percent your current mate is providing for you—or, for that matter, that this person even wants to attempt to give you the other 80 percent.

This is why it is so imperative to understand what the 80/20 rule is trying to teach. The creators of the 80/20 rule probably didn't consider this, but look at things this way: in short, this principle serves as a warning against any emotion-filled rash actions that may result in the untimely termination of a good thing, namely your relationship. Before you step outside of your unit, think about what you stand to lose. Really think about it. Is the perceived temporary alleviation of that 20 percent itch worth losing a good person who covers your ass 80 percent of the time? Are you going to let your emotions rule the way you operate? We've discussed, in length, the outcome of actions derived from a cloudy brain manipulated by the heart and little head. That 20 percent may look delicious tonight, but what about the following morning? What happens when the intoxication of lust leaves your system and all you're left with is the emotional hangover of regret? Is that surefire 80 percent worth an unsure 20 percent?

Be smart about this. If you've survived this long with a person who really cares about you, how can a new person actually compete? That new person hasn't put in the time and effort to get to know you the same way that your current mate has. They don't know your ins and outs. They don't know your passions, your fears, your life goals. They don't know your quirky side. They've never seen you at your worst. At best, this new person, with their unspoken promise to fulfill your 20 percent deficit, doesn't know enough about you to have even progressed that deeply into the Friendship phase . . . if they've made it that far at all.

You do remember the phases don't you?

The entire first phase is dedicated to finding out if you're anything other than Bust-Down material. This phase is mainly ruled by the superficial thought processes, which means Mr. Would-Be 20 Percent doesn't know a fraction of the information about you that your current lover does. Even if his silver tongue verbalizes otherwise, metaphysics and poetic vernacular doth not a strong relationship make. At the risk of sounding too raw, let's put it this way: to him you're a piece of meat with a name and cute physical characteristics at this point.

Vultures and Vulnerability

Do not underestimate the seductive power of the player-types, and do not underestimate just how much you display your discontentment for the world to see. A lot of people claim to be able to hide their feelings, but most don't even realize they wear their feelings like a brand-new blazer. Body language is a better snitch than an FBI informant. The players can zero in on your insecurities like vultures circling over a dying desert beast.

That's what players do. They watch. They gather information about you, from you. Then they use that information for personal gain. They'll find out about the absent 20 percent in your relationship you wish you had. They'll become that 20 percent—the epitome of that 20 percent. It'll be all fantasy and fairy tales. You'll believe that this temporary 20 percent can outlast your concrete 80 percent. You'll hope beyond hope that you're making the right decision, even though your brain is telling you otherwise. Once the player has had their fill, then what? You had a 20 percent excursion that could potentially damage or destroy a union with a decent person.

If someone seems too good to be true, wait it out and see. Smooth talk and fantasy are like balm to chapped lips in the winter, a temporary fix. Remember what a real soul mate is. Reject your childlike want to be swept off of your feet, because relationship magic is very rarely instantaneous. Think critically and examine the facts. You've got a lover who's put in time, made the effort, and worked to create something with you. On the other side, you have someone brand new and shiny, with no road miles. Who are you really going to trust?

Your Grass Is Always Greenest

Even if you feel unsatisfied at the moment, your grass is always greenest to you. Well, why is that? The situation you're in at the moment is always better for you than some hypothetical situation, because it's real. You have control over the life you're living. However, you cannot and do not have a bit of control over a situation you're not currently involved in. The best you can have is hope.

You can actively work on improving that 80 percent relationship. With communication and dedication to each other, you and your mate can work on the lacking 20 percent. Some people think that having an 80 percent relationship is somehow settling. This is so far from the truth. Being a part of a relationship like this isn't a bad thing. First of all, you two have proved that you can last, at least up to this point, and have a high percentage of happiness and contentment. Secondly, because relationships require constant work and time, you two should always be working to improve on something that's already pretty damn impressive.

The idea of "80 percent" is not to showcase what's missing. It is to highlight what you have. Look at it this way: The person or people who feel they have a "perfect" relationship oftentimes think they have no work to do to grow and maintain that relationship. These people can become complacent and settled, and real problems can arise. They may begin to take their mate for granted. They may forget to do the things they originally did to catch their mate. Because they erroneously believe in the perfection of their relationship, they may not put in the work to keep it thriving.

To say you have an 80 percent relationship is to acknowledge how great of a union it is, yet you're still reminding yourself that nothing is perfect and even the best relationships can be improved upon. Adhering to this thought process is the adult way to do things. We work constantly at everything else in our lives, right? Then why would it surprise anyone that a fairy tale approach to relationships—that is, expecting things to naturally be perfect—isn't the way to go? Relationships are work; the amount of mutual hustle you two put in will ultimately determine the type of relationship you have.

CHAPTER 4

REASONABLE EXPECTATIONS

SELF, RESPECT, REASONABLE EXPECTATIONS

Reasonable Expectations should have been the literary sequel to the Charles Dickens classic. Then maybe, just maybe, so many of our brains wouldn't be nursing an unhealthy, fairy tale–induced, fantasy-laced high in regard to how real-world relationships work. Seriously, it's like our whole generation has overdosed on ridiculous chick flicks, Disney princess movies, and the occasional snort of sappy greeting cards. Oh, and let's not forget about the hyper-romanticized ideas of love in 97 percent of the R&B songs we hear on the radio, constantly drilling ludicrous notions of a near-perfect love interest serving you on hand and foot. To this day, no one has actually been able to package up the sun, moon, and stars and give that gift to their dearest love.

We have been hoodwinked, friends. Relationships do not work the way we see them on the sitcoms. Issues aren't solved in twenty-seven minutes with time for two commercial station interruptions. Star-crossed lovers are a damn-near nonexistent possibility, and love at first sight mostly happens between a guy and his Philly cheesesteak sandwich . . . You're not going to be magically awoken from a mundane existence by a mysterious stranger, who just so happens to have *every* single quality you think you want in a mate.

By now, even before browsing the pages of this manual, you should be aware of the fact that no one is perfect, not even Jennifer Lopez, Brad Pitt, or Halle Berry. No, not even Halle.

The Laundry List

Do you know what the laundry list is? We've all created one at least once during our respective dating careers. And no, it has nothing to do with detergent and dyer softener sheets. The laundry list is either a physical or mental list of attributes and characteristics someone must have in order for you to consider dating them. This compilation of qualities can range from the uber-superficial to the internally meaningful. The qualities can span from the really general to the microscopically specific. There are only two universal constants for every single list.

One, these lists are totally person specific, meaning that your list isn't going to exactly mirror the next guy's. Sure, certain coveted characteristics are widespread. Everyone likes a mouth full of straight teeth. No one wants a guy who can't hold on to a job. But, your laundry list will be tailored specifically to the unique person you are.

Secondly, without fail, there isn't a laundry list in existence that can ever be perfectly met. Why is this? Simple. Our compiled list of wanted qualities, though specific to us, comes from a place of pure hope. No one hopes for an 87 percent. We hope for flawless, we hope for impeccable, we hope for the impossible. We want perfection manifested into human form, somehow forgetting that being human means, well, not being perfect at all. But we'll continue to look. That mirage of a person must be out there somewhere, right? All the while, we'll walk past good people, scarcely acknowledging their existence at all.

When faced with the question of describing the perfect mate, no one will ask for the caring girl with the drinking problem. No one will ask for the good guy with a lazy eye and receding hairline. Why? Because when we wish for something, that hope originates in the superficial centers of our thoughts. Remember, you're not forced to learn about the real person until you've taken them through the dating phases. This includes being exposed to the positive as well as negative aspects of their character. Your rational portion of the brain kicks in once you've reached the Friendship phase and you're evaluating the possibility of truly being with someone. You can't really process the idea of being with a compiled list of qualities, because this is only an idea, and you can't take ideas through the dating phases. They're not in the least bit tangible. They're basically your imagination, hence the reason you can cook up the perfect person, and why that person would reside solely in your superficial thoughts.

Anyhoo, we create an outline of characteristics we want someone to have. We embed this list into our brains. This list accompanies us everywhere we go. Regardless of whether or not you know it, you compare everyone you meet to this list of characteristics. If you have even the most remote interest in the person, a little green light goes off in your head telling the little judgment fairies to evaluate the prospect in front of you. Clearly, because you haven't had any interaction with the person other than spotting them, the fairies can focus only on the superficial items on your list. You subconsciously check off every one of these things until this person has successfully met your visually aesthetic protocol.

It is not until they've passed your preliminary (superficial) exam that you'll allow them to proceed to more evaluation, more mental poking and prodding, which is, of course, the advancement through the dating phases.

The problem with a lot of us is that we hold our potential mate wish lists to too strict a standard. Some of us truly shoot ourselves in our respective lower appendages because we'll cut someone off for maybe missing one or two qualifications on a quality checklist of a thousand items. We'll throw away a chance with a great person because we have it drilled into our brains that we need that 100 percent. Finding a perfect person is about as likely as getting struck by lightning, while drinking unicorn tears, in the middle of a storm that drops jellybeans from the heavens.

It's sad to say, but many people are cut off because some aspect of them isn't physically up to par with what you think you want. Who cares that this man could potentially have everything else you want, when you have a strict height requirement and he's five feet nine inches instead of six feet two inches. You may laugh as you read this, but this kind of silly, shallow decision-making does happen very often. Your internal lists have you focusing on what someone doesn't have, instead of the things a person does possess.

And these are just the physical requirements.

Self-test time. Describe all of the must-have characteristics that you want in a mate. How long did it take? How long was your list of attributes? Go back and reread it. Be honest with yourself. Which of these must-have characteristics are rooted securely in the superficial portions of your brain? Is every single quality a necessity in finding a good mate?

What's Reasonable?

Expectations extend much further than wanting someone to look a certain way. In short, every expectation you have for the person you may see yourself dating is a part of an equation. If he has this, and this, and this, and definitely this, that equals security. We need security in what they look like. We need security in how they can provide, and we need security in how they treat us, which includes sexual security. People being honest with themselves, entering into the dating world, need to realize this. They're going to be both the evaluator and the person being graded.

Because of this, reasonable expectations need to be implemented. The first thing everyone needs to understand is the obvious fact that no one is perfect. You're more often than not going to have to modify those laundry lists a bit, especially if you hope to find someone to be happy with, because no one's going to score a 1600 on their DATs (Dating Aptitude Test).

In order to foster reasonable expectations when dating, you need to really ask yourself a few questions. Namely, how to break down that laundry list into three categories. Of all the attributes you have listed, they'll either fall under "Needs," "Wants," or "Icing on the Cake." It is up to you to place each one of the attributes on your list into one of these categories. When you meet someone, mentally take note of the characteristics they have, and where you'd place those characteristics based on importance. Or you can write everything down if you're that anal.

"Needs" are pretty self-explanatory. These are a list of highly important qualities. Missing even one of these would be a very detrimental thing to your potential mate's overall likability. Something like "has respect for his elders" should be in this category, unless you're an ass too, and you happen to hate the elderly. Superficial shit like "has good hair" wouldn't make it into this category, unless of course you're shallow like a drying rain puddle.

"Wants" are those qualities that have a high level of significance, but not having one isn't an automatic deal breaker. You would like her to love animals, but if you never rescue that poodle from the humane society, you're not necessarily going to leave her. "Wants" are things that are important to you, but not so much that you'd cancel someone over . . . like if he had a smaller-than-desired Johnson, right? Right?

"Icing on the Cake" is everything else. "Wow, he's got a bad-ass ride." Stuff like that applies here.

The Expectation Breakdown can be imagined as follows:

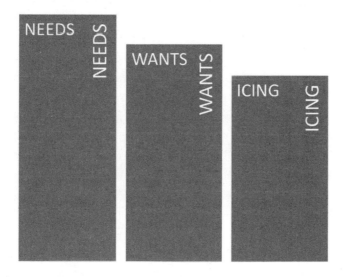

As you can see from the complicated image above, the three types of attributes your potential mate can possess have been separated. The larger the rectangle, the more important it is. So "Needs" would clearly be more important than "Wants." It is up to you to categorize by the importance of the attribute. For example, if you absolutely need this guy to be family oriented, then that particular quality goes into the "Needs" list.

Then what you do is analyze how many of each attribute your interest has, and where exactly those qualities are categorized. Let's say the guy has 150 qualities you absolutely need, 150 of his other attributes fall under "Wants," and he has five "Icing on the Cake" elements. You had a total of 305 qualities on your laundry list. Based on the breakdown, he has a lot of things you really need from him, and just as many things you want. He even has a few extras, like power windows and heated seats.

Based on the data you've gathered and categorized, you should have a clearer picture, at least from your point of view, about how your would-be mate ranks on your internal scale. This method forces you to look inside yourself as you define which attributes are important to have in a mate. You'll clearly see just how superficial you can be in the dating selection process based on the attributes you've chosen and where exactly those qualities fall on your expectation scale.

Hopefully, you'll gain a clearer picture of your dating choices. Are you moved by superficial elements, or are you more drawn to the personality makeup of a person? More importantly, you should be able to identify your dating patterns. If you're successful in dating, maybe you need to tweak your expectation breakdown slightly. If you've been stinking up the dating game for a while, this is a chance to have your thoughts categorized, right in front of you. You can reevaluate how you pick a mate. You can reevaluate what attributes are important and how important they are, and then adjust according to previous experience. If you're always going for the muscle-head, asshole jock, then maybe rock-hard pectorals shouldn't be in your "Needs" category.

Appreciate the fact that you're being analyzed by your potential mate as well. They may not be as sophisticated as you, because you're using our nifty expectation divider, but they do run you through a laundry list of items they need or want you to have. It is difficult earlier on to know why someone has an interest in you. Most people are just happy that they can grab someone's attention to begin with. But, unless you like being a piece of meat, you should not want to be around someone who likes you only for superficial reasons. The saying is "Time reveals all the snakes," or something like that. Truth is, actions reveal the snakes. If your love interest's interactions with you are mainly of the superficial nature—that is, they want you for sex, or as a hot accessory on their arm—then their expectations of you are rooted in the shallow. Another clue that their expectations don't deal in the substantial is that they don't explore anything deeper with you. You guys won't be visiting museums, or having meaningful conversations, or even communicating all that much to begin with. Pay attention, and you'll begin to understand where this type of person's real interest rests.

Fair-Dating Procedure

Having a standard operating procedure for your dating life isn't necessarily a bad thing, unless of course you keep repeating the same negative patterns over and over, getting the same empty results. Some dating guidelines make perfect sense, like getting to know someone before pulling your dick out and playing target practice. Demanding a certain level of respect is another. Going Dutch on the bills until everything's official is one more. Even cooperative planning of the dates makes perfect sense. Some people, however, like to pull out that inner diva, those unfair guidelines that do nothing more than display your selfishness, and, in some cases, utter hypocrisy.

Having reasonable expectations in a potential mate is key to keeping that person around. You need a healthy balance of give-and-take. You don't want to be an armed forces general, demanding things from your would-be boo, but at the same time, you can't let them step all over you either. Reasonable expectations come from the mutual understanding that both of you are individuals with your own respective problems, responsibilities, fears, goals, and lives. If you want your relationship to flourish, you cannot allow all of your issues to take precedence over theirs. As a matter of fact, one could argue that the best relationships work when you put your mate's needs above your own, and they in turn do the same for you. Fair dating can be achieved simply by taking into account the person you're dating.

The Hypocritical Dater

For instance, some people expect their love interests to treat them like royalty, when they're constantly treating their dates like subjects. Yeah, yeah, maybe you were the hot bitch in high school, because the people clawing and scratching and pulling themselves toward your unattainable affections didn't know any better. That crap doesn't fly in the here and now. You know why? Because if the tables were reversed, the diva wouldn't be able to handle it. Jesus said it, Buddha said it, and a whole multitude of enlightened individuals preach to treat others the way you want to be treated. This is in all realms, including love and relationships. But alas, some people are taught to act the opposite way.

The dating game is quite the psychological chess match. Many people engage in mind games in order to give themselves a dysfunctional sense of security. They'll do things to test the other person's resolve, to see if their potential mate wants to really be in the picture. Frankly, this kind of shit is dated and played. When someone likes you, truly likes you, they're going to show you in the best way they know how. You don't need to have them jumping through unnecessary hoops, especially when you wouldn't lace up your own cross-trainers to run through their perceptual obstacle course.

Don't do dumb shit like the cliché making your partner jealous . . . on purpose. Now, if you're dealing with someone who has trust issues, or some sort of self-esteem problem, they could be developing unwarranted jealousy because their foggy brain is telling them to. However, to go out of your way to parade other would-be suitors in your potential mate's face is, for lack of a better term, fucked up.

Here's a clue. If they're dating you, clearly they believe there are things attractive about you that make you D8able. They wouldn't be going out with you if they didn't. Seriously, who tries to meet someone they're not attracted to in order to go out with them? This isn't some '90s-era chick flick. Testing their level of jealousy actually shows a flawed self-esteem you're carting around inside that dysfunctional head of yours. If you're trying this childish game plan with a potential mate who's confident and secure, they'll probably end up leaving. No grown person who's really trying to show another person they care is going to take kindly to this treatment. It's an emotional slug to the chin. But hey, you have a parade of would-be suitors at your disposal, right . . . ?

The bottom line is, engaging in negative actions against people to purposely elicit a response is just wrong. You know going in that these actions have the capacity to, at the least, piss someone off. They could very well cause a lot of pain and anxiety for your potential mate. Willfully manipulating someone into doing what you want them to do shows that you don't really care about them as a person. You're totally disregarding their feelings, and you're just plain selfish. You know very well that if the shoe were on the other foot, or the table were turned another 180 degrees, you'd be butt-hurt too. When we talk about reasonable expectations, like everything else in relationships, it's a two-way street. There is nothing reasonable about shitty mind games. Nothing but mental exhaustion and relationship failure can come out of these types of games.

Please, please, please avoid trying to change the person you're going out with. A lot of you out there liken yourselves to a building contractor or construction worker. You think you can meet someone, find out about certain characteristics you don't like, tear this person down, and rebuild them as you see fit. You cannot change someone you met, especially not with those adolescent games previously described. It takes an arrogant person to think they can and need to change someone else's qualities. If you don't like the guy that much, let him walk. Refocus on you and keep hunting, because it's pretty much a guarantee that you wouldn't allow someone to erase parts of you and plug in their "upgrades."

Princess Complexes and Other Debacles

Probably one of the deadliest killers in all social interaction is the idea of the Princess. Maybe it's Disney. Maybe the cause stems from someone's parents filling their heads with absolute drivel. Originally thought to be predominantly a female sickness, we have come to learn that the princess complex can overtake anyone. The seed is planted when you're young. It starts out as a simple idea, then it eventually germinates. The vines of inflated self-worth begin to choke the living sense out of the poor victim. Some people go on for years living with this terrible fungus corrupting the brain, pushing out common sense. If left unchecked, the princess complex can affect the victim in every aspect of their life. Only a good, firm smack from reality can clear up the infection. Sometimes people need multiple doses of reality shots because the fungus has just grown so deeply.

Being a Princess is essentially having this idea in your head that you are somehow better than everyone else around you. There isn't any real evidence to back it up, but you believe it through and through. Believed to be brought on by early-onset parental babying and spoiling, the princess complex can severely retard normal social interaction. The delusional belief that you are the exception to many of the social norms is the first sign of someone suffering from the princess complex.

In terms of dating and relationships, these are the people who act as though they somehow transcend the give-and-take of a normal relationship. They feel not only that they deserve to be catered to, but also as if the person or people doing the catering should feel honored to be allowed to accommodate. They revel in the one-sided relationship, because, well, they're them and you should treat them like the royalty they feel they are in their own respective minds. The Princess believes that reasonable expectations don't apply to them. They want the best mate possible, without even considering that they might need to also be the best mate possible. The Princess is the ultimate example of the hypocritical dater because they truly believe that they are immune to the negativity of relationships, while spreading that very negativity themselves.

If this is you . . . get ready for that dose of reality.

If left unchecked, the Princess has a tragic end waiting for them. You see, a Princess is a fairy tale figure, and we live in the real world. Reality has a way of washing all that glass-slipper, seven-servants, talking-animal shit down the drain. Because the Princess believes themselves to be above others, said Princess doesn't learn how to operate socially. The Princess expects everyone and everything to be placed on a bed of roses at their feet. While this may actually work out at first, the Princess's reign never lasts forever. Why is that? Let's explore the Princess's life a bit.

From the time when Their Highness is very young, they are given almost everything they want. They never learn how to work for things. More importantly, they don't know how to socially interact with others in order to negotiate for the things they want . . . And why should they, when everything is handed to them? For a time, life is quite grand. Everything, including suitors, just fall right into Highness's lap.

The Princess is also constantly being told how they are somehow better than others with no valid proof given to support the outrageous claims of their greatness. They grow up, and having been catered to for so long, they have not learned how to do so for themselves. They have been mentally and socially separated from average folks who have to work for everything they get . . . be it money, be it a job, or be it a dick with a good guy attached. They have not learned the careful balancing act of the cat-and-mouse game. The Princess has never had to play the chess game up to this point.

Eventually, reality sets in. The world sucks Little Miss Storybook out of the fairy tale and into the real-world dating game. Because the Princess has been brainwashed with the "I'm better than you" ideology, Highness hasn't had to learn the ins and outs, the highs and lows, or the positives and negatives of dating and how to look out for these aspects. Highness also doesn't realize that isolation from the commoners has rendered the Princess pretty useless in reading other people. The Princess is much more susceptible to a smooth talker than someone who's learned through experience to spot the fakes and catch the nice ones.

Also, it should be noted that because of the social barrier kept between the Royal Highness and the commoners, it's much more difficult for the Princess to move out of the Bust-Down Worthy phase in the suitor's eyes, because of the difficulty in getting to know the Princess. People with genuine interests will become fewer and fewer, with the threat of only vultures remaining. Essentially, years and years of the delusional "better than you" worldview can actually push decent people away. The unreasonable expectations brought forth by the Princess's laundry list of necessary mate attributes, fused with the Princess's inability to read and interact with people accordingly, will ultimately lead to the Highness's fall from grace. They'll be contending with people who talk the right game but can't showcase the moves, and be missing out on the less-than-perfect commoner who may have treated the Princess amazingly.

How does the Princess avoid becoming lost and turned out? Highness needs to understand that the majority of the fairy tales spoon-fed to them are crap. You're no better than anyone else, and eventually the world will show you this. Get smart and get proactive socially, especially in the dating game. Don't fall victim to the lies your parents told you when you were too young to understand them anyway.

Origins of Unreasonable Expectations

Clearly, the fairy tales sold to you by your parents are from an origin of unreasonable expectations. Don't be a Princess. There is no perfect Prince Charming out there. TV, movies, books, and other forms of media also add to our collective thought process in regard to finding the perfect mate. But, none of these avenues would exist if it weren't for the abundance of people with self-esteem issues tied into dating and relationships.

Make no mistake, the princess complex is also rooted in a self-esteem deficiency—your parents'. The parent who brainwashes their kid to be a Princess is probably trying to compensate for something that happened in their past. So, in a dysfunctional way, they're trying to protect their children, ultimately retarding them socially, but trying to protect them all the same.

Unreasonable expectations are the extreme assumption that things will go perfectly in your favor. When this thought process is applied to another person, namely in relationships, it is the extreme assumption that this person will be perfect on a number of levels. You already know about the physical attributes. They're self-explanatory. When one person exacts unreasonable expectations on another, they are basically expecting that other person to plug each and every hole that exists in their life. This is why the idea of reasonable and unreasonable expectations varies from relationship to relationship, because everyone's life is different. The common thread, however, with unreasonable expectations is the pursuit of that person who can perfectly cover your imperfections. Coincidentally, an imperfect person can be your match in that regard, but as explained earlier, the superficial portion of your brain isn't going to construct a 93 percent perfect person.

Over-the-top requirements involved in the search for your other half are arguably tied into your self-esteem in one of two ways. Your self-esteem could be so unrealistically high, like in the case of a Princess, that you expect a perfect mate to match what you consider to be perfect . . . ummm, yourself. Or, your self-esteem could be so beat to shit that you want someone you perceive to have it totally together, to latch on to.

Unrealistic, sky-high self-esteem can be matched only by the want for an unrealistic, perfect mate. Those who apply for the position with the princess complex types better be ready for serious scrutiny. In these people's minds, because the Princess is perfect, they'll need a mate just as perfect as them. But, because no one actually is perfect, good luck with getting into and staying in a Princess's good graces. The would-be suitor's repeated failure to live up to perfection serves as fortification for the delusional thought that no one is ever really good enough for the Princess. The slick vultures out there, however, will be able to talk the right jargon to get what they want. You'd better believe that they don't want to get any further than the Bust-Down Worthy phase.

Those with rock-bottom self-esteem need that perfect mate for an entirely different reason. They need someone to latch on to. They need a source of happiness. They need another person to be a buffer for the crap they can't handle in their own life. The major unfair expectations usually seen in these types of relationships revolve around their insecurity. One mate will be unfairly expected to be the source of happiness for the other. As you know, true happiness is found from within, so because of this, the mate will not be able to appease their partner. This scenario makes for an emotionally one-sided relationship. A major sign that you have this sort of self-esteem deficiency, or that you're dealing with someone like this, is clinginess. Excessive clinginess, especially earlier on in the game, is a definite sign that this person is lacking something. Whatever it is that they're lacking is eating away at their self-esteem and the mate is viewed as the superglue to hold everything together. It's quite the unfair position for the potential mate to have to deal with.

Folks with healthy self-esteem don't present unreasonable guidelines to the people they date because they realize that no one is perfect. This includes them. They have come to grips with their flaws, have accepted these flaws, and have set plans in motion to improve on these flaws. People with healthy self-esteem also know the utter impossibility of finding the perfect person, and that a laundry list of qualities is a waste of time. They don't rely on another imperfect person to make them feel secure, be it in relationships or other aspects of their lives. Instead, these people, with realistic outlooks on life, focus on finding that imperfect being who fits well with them. They're not in a race against time, and ultimately they enjoy the life they're living while they're living it. In other words, life being single is great, and life will be great in a relationship. Be like these people. Work on understanding your self-worth. Work on improving you. Everything else will fall into place.

How to Increase Your Expectations . . . the Right Way

Having certain expectations in dating is natural. It makes sense to want certain things when you're dating. It makes sense to want your potential life partner to treat you a certain way. You shouldn't be accepting of negative behavior, no matter how trivial the other person thinks it is. There is a difference between understanding everyone's imperfections and settling. You should never settle. You should also definitely want your new mate to bring a level of financial, physical, emotional, and sexual stability to the table.

However . . .

If you're not bringing those things too, then you need to have more than several seats and reevaluate your life.

The audacity of some people is astounding. In the case of people suffering from the princess complex, at least they were brainwashed at a young age. What about those other folks, walking around not doing a damned thing for self-improvement? How can they possibly have the balls, or the female equivalent, to create these attribute laundry lists for other people, when they honestly wouldn't even be able to meet their own criteria? What makes them think they're worthy of a shining example of a mate? Self-entitlement is a nasty beast.

Dating is always going to be a two-way street. You get what you put in. So, if you bring nothing to the table, expect to find and deal with others who don't have much to show either. Here's another example of why dating always, always, always starts with you: Internal improvement leads to better choices, with all things. Don't be a penniless pauper hoping to score a rich guy. There's a reason rich folks are rich; they surround themselves with other rich folks. Step your earning game up. Don't live off of doughnuts and try to catch the super-healthy chick at the gym. She's probably not going to look at you twice. Ever heard the saying "Dress for the job you want"? Well, it's true, except in this case it's "Make yourself into the person you want to attract." There really is nothing you can't accomplish if you can figure out how to systematically go after what it is you want. Major life changes never happen overnight, but they do happen if you put in the work. The good news is, we can always improve on the people we are. It all starts with the want to do so, followed by the plan, then the unwavering action.

If you're legitimately putting in the time, you have the right to expect someone to do the same.

CHAPTER 5

COMMUNICATION

EMPATHY, LISTENING, EQUALITY, COMMUNICATION, FORGIVENESS, APPRECIATION, TRUST, LONGEVITY, COMMON INTERESTS

What do you believe to be the backbone of a solid relationship? Is it passion? Maybe interstellar sex with out-of-this-world equipment is what'll hold two people together for the long ride? No, no, no, it's common interests. Common interests have to be what hold a relationship together, right? Though all of these elements help in sweetening the deal, the mainstay of any successful relationship, dating or otherwise, is communication.

Without communication, the relationship wouldn't even get off the ground. Here's the thing: Relationships are a lot like plants. Plants need a number of things to thrive. The better the quality of those particular elements, the better the development of the plant. Most of the sources of nourishment can be interchangeable yet still yield similar results. You can trade in natural light for special lamps. Plants can survive with different types of soil. The one thing, however, that can't be substituted is the need for water. Go ahead. Try to pour a soft drink into your plant's soil and wait to see if that plant grows. You'll be waiting a very long time. Water is the only element in the growth and survival process of a plant that cannot be substituted for anything else. Certain death is inevitable without the constant supply of nourishment that comes only from what water can provide.

Communication is your relationship's water.

Look at any relationship. Many of the pillars needed to erect a strong union between two people are rather flexible . . . flexible in the sense that there is more than one way to build a particular pillar. Different people do varied things to show that they love and care for one another. What you do will not perfectly match up with what your mate chooses to do to illustrate an affinity for you. But, as those certain must-have needs are met (regardless of how), rapport is built and the relationship is strengthened. Communication can't rightfully be considered a pillar. It's more like the concrete center of the relationship, which all other aspects of the relationship latch on to for support. And like those plants without water, your relationship is destined to shrivel up and die without communication.

What's even funnier is the fact that the majority of intimate couplings out there do not have the strongest pillars or even the greatest communication. Have you ever seen a plant that gets less-than-optimal nourishment? It holds on as best as it can. It may not be the greenest, or the tallest, but it grabs whatever it can to stay alive. Relationships are the same way.

Many of the shortcomings in relationships aren't bad enough to end the relationship, but maybe just cripple it a bit. Relationships like these are in survival mode. There is no real growth; they kind of just run in place like those stationary bikes at gyms. There's a whole lot of work going on, but they're not really getting anywhere. Even a relationship with shitty communication can sputter along for a while, but you can very easily notice a difference between a relationship with good communication and one that suffers from a lack of quality dialogue.

Surprisingly enough, the difference between solid communication and bad communication is quite minimal. With nothing more than a few internal tweaks, you'll be a much better communicator within your intimate setup as well as in situations with folks you don't necessarily want to get naked with.

The Body, the Language

This has to be said. We are not the first to write about this, and we'll probably not be the last, but here goes . . .

Body language. You knew this was coming. All the articles, scientific journals, and editorial fluff pieces you've read that reference body language, and its importance, probably have some truth to them. Communication via body language is not a myth. People assume that stringing words together is the driving force behind communication. In actuality, conveying a verbal message is broken up into three unequal parts. Now, writers, philosophers, and other know-it-alls can argue the percentage of each portion until the sun's batteries run out. That's not what's important here. What you need to take away from this is, in fact, that the words coming out of your mouth, though powerful in their own right, are totally fueled by your state of mind at the time you say those words. Furthermore, your tone when speaking these strings of words is also affected by your state of mind. Lastly, and most importantly, your body language is the visible manifestation of what's taking place in your head.

Most people will readily accept the first two points. They seem like common sense, right? When you're happy, you sound happy. When you're pissed off, your tone and cadence as well as the words chosen will easily reflect that. However, people for whatever reason will not accept how powerful, how noticeable body language truly is. Well, it absolutely, positively is. Some hiring managers would argue that the difference between a hired candidate and a resume that's filed away for six months is the candidate's body language during the interview . . .

Look at times when your body language has clearly been at the center of your communication efforts. Have you ever been in a fight? Not a verbal argument, but have you ever been in a physical altercation where you were so enraged you saw red? You didn't have to say a word for people to know you were upset. Your muscles were tightened, your hands were probably trembling, and your eyes could cut through the two-day-old biscuits from your local chicken joint. Your body language sent the only message that needed to be sent.

Look at someone in extreme emotional pain. Aside from the crying, their head is probably lowered and their shoulders are slumped. Or, how about that arrogant guy with his perfect hair and designer shades? Those things aren't what convince you of his arrogance, however. His self-assurance is better illustrated by his chest being puffed out, his shoulders being pulled back, and the long, rhythmic strides he takes when traversing the pavement. It's almost as if he thinks those concrete slabs belong to him (the funny thing is, he may not be some arrogant prick, but his body language tells a story for whoever tries to read it). In these scenarios, not a word needed to be spoken for you to consume volumes of information on the subjects.

Yes, the abovementioned examples are extreme, but your body is firing messages out all the time to the people around you, regardless of whether or not you want to admit it.

Another aspect of body language people fail to consider is facial expression. A fake smile is a fake smile. The reason we call it a fake smile is that most people can tell it's a fake smile. A poker face wouldn't need to exist if we were naturally good at hiding emotion in our faces. Eyes give it away. The way your mouth quivers can give it away. Remember, emotion is constantly trying to manifest itself through your body, and your face is the big-screen TV.

If you agree that bodily messaging is the primary driving force in communication in general, then you have to also admit that linguistics originating from your frame are also the major component in communication throughout the stages of a relationship.

Perception Is Everything

Body language is often one of those things we see in others but don't notice in ourselves. Do not underestimate the way you carry yourself. It is quite recognizable and the first thing people notice about you before you even speak. Have you ever wondered why your seventh-grade teacher would teach you how to walk with your head up and shoulders back? You can be the most confident, capable person in the world, but if you don't carry yourself as though you are, people can misread you. Something as simple as lifting your head gives you a look of elevated confidence, which in turn makes you that much more attractive.

Being a people watcher can be a helpful tool in targeting faulty body language in yourself. Go to one of the typical grounds for nocturnal social interaction. You probably know them as "clubs" or "bars." Pay attention to the people most successful in initiating conversations. You very rarely see the hunter with slumped shoulders and drooped head getting much attention, or setting up any hookups, for that matter. The people who do well in these social settings carry themselves in such a way as to suggest that they know that they should do well. They're not fishing for attention. They're not being overly chatty, attempting to bed every person they meet. They seem confident enough and focused on themselves. When they see someone they're interested in, they go after that someone. There's no hesitation, no self-doubt, just what seems to be a natural and effortless focus to grab the attention of a potential playmate.

Perception is everything. Even if you're not the most confident person out there, a good mask of confidence can take you a long way. Fake it 'til you feel it. While you're learning to appreciate yourself, your confidence will continue to grow. At the same time, carrying yourself as though your confidence meter is already at a hundred makes a good impression on those eyeing you. So technically you're not really faking it. Think of this as an advance of royalties for the self-esteem you will be receiving shortly.

Something should be said about the dual psychological effects of acting like your self-esteem is peaking. The physical act of carrying yourself upright, with shoulders back and head up, while taking long strides actually makes you feel better about yourself. Go ahead, try it. Give it a couple of rounds in your living room. You'll feel stronger, more capable, more sure of yourself. Smiling too. The next time you're having an extra-shitty day, force and hold a smile. Seriously. See if you're not feeling better in a minimal amount of time.

Bad Communication

Communication is the giving and receiving of impressions, emotions, or knowledge through speech, written words, or, in the case of body language, gestures. Bad communication, in its simplest form, is a breakdown in understanding of the ideas, knowledge, or feelings being expressed between the recipient and the person engaging in the expression. This breakdown can happen in a number of ways, but the universal constant is the fact that, for whatever reason, the two involved just don't see eye to eye. There are probably just as many reasons for bad communication as there are people on the planet who commit the crime.

So what constitutes bad communication? Is it a simple misunderstanding, or a lack of willingness to listen? Is it a lack of sympathy from one or both parties involved? In relationships, bad communication at its core isn't necessarily a lack of caring for the other person. Less-than-optimal interconnectivity in a relationship stems from a certain level of selfishness from one or both parties involved. This doesn't necessarily mean the selfishness is rooted in something malicious or evil. It could very well be because the selfish folks haven't learned how to take others into account. Yes, this is something that actually needs to be learned and put into practice.

Less-than-stellar communication does not have to do only with times you're fighting with your mate. Bad communication can encompass all aspects of your relationship. Even during the good times, lack of communication isn't a good thing. It shows that you don't consider the other person's feelings regarding certain things. Granted, some things may not be any of their business, but when you're in a relationship with a caring soul, they want to know as much as possible about you, including the good times.

This can be hard for certain types of people to adjust to. Some people just aren't good at opening up and sharing personal things. If you've ever been the guarded type, you can understand how difficult it can be to share anything. Getting over this roadblock will be crucial to improving your communication.

Someone can be an all-around nice person. They can donate to charities, help old folks cross the street, and even save little kittens from trees. This does not mean, however, that they'll naturally know how to conduct themselves productively in a relationship. Take, for instance, a person who's been single for quite a while, then suddenly ends up in a new dating setting with a new person. Being single allows you to be selfish—well, selfish in the relationship realm because you have no intimate relationship to foster. Suddenly, selfishness is expected to be thrown out of the window and replaced by empathy toward a new cluster of emotions, as well as new fears, needs, and wants along with your own. It can be, and often is, a shock to the system.

There is no learning curve, and we all respond differently in our roles in relationships. Remember, everything is relative, and what you perceive to be bad communication may be what the next person thinks is demanding way too much in the sharing department. Not to mention, we are all the sum of our previous experiences, and communication between two people is definitely one of those indicators of compatibility. Those experiences can cause one to be closed off from others, untrusting, or a whole number of other social variations. Better communication, however, is something that can be learned over time . . . And what do you know, we'll be discussing that shortly.

With all that being said, and now that playing devil's advocate is out of the way . . . some people can just be selfish dicks. Bad communication can be one of the indicators of their rather phallic personalities, but may not be enough alone to crucify them. There are usually a number of indicators that would suggest this person isn't right for you. Hey, after your self-exploration you may realize that you're the asshole. Hopefully, this manual will be the spark that pushes you toward being less of that prick.

The Reasons . . . That We're Here

No, not the famous song. The reasons behind bad communication all come from either an inability for someone to effectively get their point across, or the inability of the recipient to grasp the message being sent. In total clusterfucks, both sides are inept at passing and receiving messages . . . If you want an example of this, check out any bipartisan government, anywhere.

Bad communication is the failure to see an issue through the other person's eyes. Remember that one of the true signs of caring for another is attempting to do just that, to see an issue from another person's position. One would think that this is an easy task, but it's not always the case. Everyone is different. You may think the issue at hand is stupid, or trivial. They may not feel the same way. Your position on an issue, your personal experiences, and your preferences all play a part in where you'll stand in a potential disagreement. This is normal. This is expected. It is what you decide to do because of this difference in opinion that will show the type of communicator you are.

Right and Wrong

We're not always going to agree. Arguments are commonplace in any relationship, good or bad. There is, however, a right way to go about participating in a disagreement. There is clearly a flawed way to take part in an argument as well.

Pointing fingers, getting loud, and refusing to take responsibility for your part in the disagreement are all elements of the wrong way to argue. Even if your partner is dead wrong, taking an unnecessary offensive approach to handling the situation does not diffuse it. If anything, you're tossing a few more sticks of dynamite on an already explosive set of circumstances. This is bad communication, which if done too frequently will aid in developing a negative cycle of communication.

But, this seems to be the mode of operation for most people during an argument. Selfishness at its finest. An individual can become so wrapped up in how *they* feel that they forget about the other person. Sure, emotions can run high and extremely hot during an altercation, especially an altercation with a loved one (probably because you're wondering how someone so close to you could be such an idiot about [fill in the blank]). You can't help how you feel, this is true, but you can help how those feelings are manifested during your back-and-forth with your mate.

Remember, perception is everything. The way you present your side of the story really can make the difference between causing a little ripple and a monstrous tsunami of emotion. Swearing or calling the other person a derogatory name is way too offensive, and it's damn disrespectful. If you want someone to shut down almost immediately, do something like this.

Hmmm, let's see. Not listening in an argument is another huge gaffe. Being present in the room during an argument does not constitute listening. Zoning out while the other person spews their hateful rhetoric, only to then sling your razor-sharp insults, isn't listening. You're just waiting for your turn to return the diss.

Bringing in third parties is just plain dumb. Don't you dare ever say something like, "Well, Gina sees my point of view." What the fuck does Gina have to do with an argument between you and your significant other? Nothing of importance, so keep your personal business out of the ears and minds of your friends. If you must tell someone, don't tell your significant other you divulged to another person . . . And you better be sure this Gina girl can keep her trap shut, or you're asking to seriously compound an already sensitive issue.

Probably the worst thing—*the worst* thing—you can do is point the finger at someone. "This is all your fault" has destroyed many a relationship. There are always two to tango, regardless of whether or not both of you are dancing over a pile of horseshit. Even if in your heart of hearts, you feel that this person is wrong, unless you want to severely damage your bond, refrain from placing the total of any sort of blame on them.

The way you say things, in general, needs to be . . . ummm . . . filtered, if you will. Your body language can't seem combative (don't swell up like the Incredible Hulk when you argue). There is a whole host of actions you need to stay away from. Keep this in mind as we discuss . . .

The right way to argue. The correct way to go about getting your point across in a disagreement is *not* to engage in any of the aforementioned stupidity. The easiest way to go about carrying yourself correctly in an argument is to remember one thing: the person whose throat you're considering ripping out actually cares about you. Miscommunication or not, at some level, they do care. Because of this, you need to give them some leniency.

Keep calm. Treat this scenario like a job interview. You want to show your mate the best you. Listen to what they have to say. No, really listen. Don't just wait for your turn to talk. Really absorb what they're trying to say. Regardless of how hurtful it may sound, you set the precedent with your maturity. When it is your turn to talk, don't go the low route and start the blame game all over again. Be an adult and acknowledge the part you played in the current shit-symphony. Be open and honest when discussing what your issues are. Do not, repeat, do not point fingers. Ask questions instead of making definite, negative statements about your partner.

If this isn't a deal-breaking argument, and most of them aren't, make certain that you assure your significant other that you still care about them. If the argument seems as if it's heating up, back away until the boiling subsides. Remember, this person cares about you, so don't treat them like an enemy. Get your emotions in order and you'll be looking forward to the makeup sex instead of the rebound booty.

You'll find that this route works infinitely better than the alternative. When you're calm, you invite the other person to be calm too. Also, when people are calmer, they tend to think a lot more clearly. Anger, when left to make decisions, usually makes terrible ones. Remember, visceral emotion comes from the heart. The heart doesn't do a good job of communicating. Your brain, on the other hand, is the originator of rational thought. In times of extreme emotion, do not forget your brain and the role it plays in getting your heart to sit the hell down and chill the hell out.

Fighting Bad Communication

What does bad communication look like? No one is perfect, and you're bound to have moments of miscommunication. These moments aren't an indication of true bad communication. They're indications, instead, of the fact that no one is exactly alike, and in a relationship, you may have to find different ways to communicate in order to keep things moving smoothly. Random times of miscommunication are also indicators that relationships will always need some level of work because they do not exist in perfect harmony any more than the two involved are flawless beings.

So don't get scared because you can think back to a few times when you and your significant other had bouts with miscommunication. Everyone does. And if you're single right now, don't worry. Even after you meet that perfect mate, you too will have disagreements that originate from some sort of miscommunication. It is what it is. The way you handle these instances will ultimately determine what sort of back-and-forth you'll have with your significant other.

The cycle of bad communication looks a little something like this:

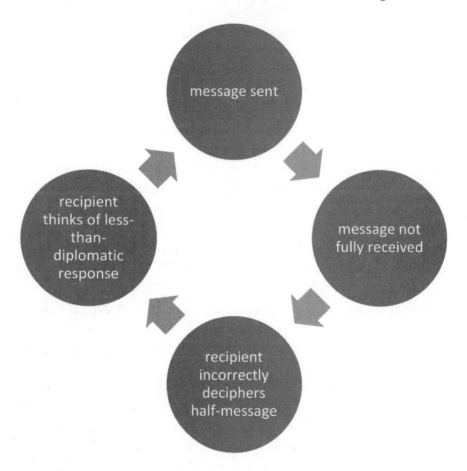

As you can see, the cycle of bad communication begins with a particular message not being fully understood. If you can recall, the message isn't absorbed because of the selfishness of the recipient. Instead of the recipient trying to see through their significant other's point of view, they internalize what portions of the message they managed to absorb. Most likely, because the recipient hasn't learned to see their mate's point of view, they'll make the assumption that the message is an attack.

The wounded recipient will then think of a response based on how the original message made them feel. Because the response is most likely chock-full of emotion, the heart had a bigger part in creating it. The brain just made sure the words were pronounced right, if that. Anyhoo . . . the recipient thinks of something snappy to say. Then the neurons fire off an equally questionable response to the original messenger.

The messenger, now the recipient, will most likely be offended by the other party's response. Thus, the cycle of bad communication is created. Even in scenarios where a disagreement isn't involved, bad communicators have a way of not fully grasping each other's messages. It's kind of like that childhood game, "Telephone": A message gets passed down a line of little kids. By the time it reaches the last kid, the message has totally changed. Well, bad communicators are a lot like a bunch of little kids with short attention spans. They really don't care as much about the message as they do about being able to respond to the message.

There should be no wonder then why so many conversations are miscommunicated and why so many arguments end up exploding. People are too selfish to learn a little tact in what they say, and people are also too selfish to give others the benefit of the doubt when a message sounds like it flew out of left field. Simply remembering that you care about your significant other can go a long way.

Good Communication

This . . . is the main support structure for any successful relationship. It holds everything together. Communication truly is the backbone of your relationship. Everything else about your union grows out of the type of communication you have. Without it, you're as good as dead. Well, the relationship is as good as dead. There really isn't some secret formula for concocting good communication. There is no alchemy involved. The foundation for good communication is a rather simple idea. It is the idea that you need to see your relationship through your partner's eyes. Are the things you're communicating, or not communicating, bound to hurt them in some way? In other words, if your partner conveyed messages to you in the same way you communicate with them, would you be upset?

In a previous chapter, we discussed the key components to making a relationship run smoothly. One of the major elements to doing this is to put your significant other's needs ahead of your own, knowing that they'll do the same for you. If both parties were to consent to this behavior, then theoretically, neither partner would ever want for a thing. Well, the need for solid communication in a relationship is probably one of the most—if not the most—important needs.

Being a good communicator isn't something that happens overnight. Even children have to learn to speak their native tongues over time. But, by keeping your partner's needs at the forefront, you can do nothing but improve in the communication department. It really is just a matter of sustained selflessness in dealing with your mate. Do not think, however, that your relationship will always run smoothly. Your relationship will never be perfect, but through good communication, you'll be able to handle any bumps in the road.

Always remember that communication doesn't just involve you sharing information with your partner. It encompasses how you share that information as well. Body language and tone are essential to getting your point across in a calm, noncombatant fashion. Equally as important is how well you receive the information being shared with you. Communication is also about the ability to listen and understand. You're not just waiting for your turn to talk. Finally, good communication, especially in heated moments, is about giving your partner the benefit of the doubt. It's about remembering, above all else, that you two care for each other.

CHAPTER 6

COMMON INTERESTS

LONGEVITY, COMMON INTERESTS, RESPECT, COMMUNICATION

Consider this one of the first bricks added to the construction of your relationship. Common interests. These are much more than a series of events and outings that you enjoy doing with your potential mate. One could argue that common interests are what catapult you out of the Bust-Down Worthy phase and land you somewhere squarely in the Friendship phase. These are what separate people you're just interested in fucking from those who have the potential to be something more than the eye candy you want to taste. Common interests are the catalyst for wanting to gather deeper information about your new buddy; they are the turning point, the little switch in your brain that weans you off of the superficial way of thinking.

Go back to the chapter "The Superficial Gay: Intimacy." If you can recall, the initial stages of attraction are fueled by the superficial parts of our brains. Through rapport building and the seeking of deeper information, we begin to develop more value for the new love interest. Remember, initially, superficial is all we can be with the potential mate because we don't have any other substantial information to go on. They caught your eye. You think they're attractive. You may want to bed them.

It is not until you have your initial exchange of words that you begin to develop a rapport. This rapport is still rooted in the superficial mind-set, however, but it is this initial conversation that'll clue you in to whether or not this person has the potential to be more than just eye-fuckable. If this initial interaction goes well, numbers are exchanged, and you go from there.

The conversations leading up to the first date are still superficial, but you begin to learn things about each other that are slightly deeper than the aesthetic information you gathered from your eyes' reconnaissance. Enter common interests . . .

By definition, common interests are the things you both are into. But they also play a much deeper role than you may realize. They are not just excursions, restaurants, movies, and extracurricular activities you share a mutual liking for. Common interests are the first form of substantial mutual discovery between you and a potential mate. They are your first activity together as a duo, and a very substantial one at that. When you begin conversing with your newfound love candidate, you're almost in a sense interviewing them to see if they'll have an important place in your life. Common interests are the first indicator of whether or not this can happen.

Think about the first few conversations you may have. Sure, you may be gathering information to plan out the first date, but more importantly, you two are feeling each other out. You're actively looking for solid, common ground. Those three-hour conversations during the twilight hours aren't just to kill time. The euphoria you feel, or the butterflies, if you will, is the exciting revelation that you two are connecting through something much deeper than a physical attraction. With every shared commonality, an emotional twine is bound between the two of you. That twine is attached at the heart and runs through your brain. The more of these twines you create, the stronger the bond.

Common Interests and Rapport Building

The first stage of rapport building within the Friendship phase is built totally from common interests. Secondary attraction (interest other than sex) would not exist without the discovery of common interests early on. You two have just met, and you have the brand-new-person smell on each of you. Maybe it's rooted in the subconscious, maybe there's some sort of science to it, but people naturally tend to lean toward learning favorable information about each other in the beginning. It builds a level of comfort between the two involved. This level of comfort leads to the want to explore even more about each other. Again, maybe it's your subconscious compelling you, but you begin to find the common links with the new information you're gathering about your potential mate. With every commonality you find between you two, the more favorable the rapport becomes. There is no set schedule for the satisfactory building of the rapport, but make no mistake, without the successful development of this level of rapport, the relationship would surely stall. For a number of reasons, it is in the best interest of you two to find as many excursions, restaurants, movies, and extracurricular activities you both enjoy.

Once you two have reached the Friendship phase, the strength of your rapport will be based on the volume of common interests you have. In the beginning, the common interests will be very shallow. Most of the common interests will be physical in nature. For example, you two may find that you share the same affinity for rock climbing or certain museums. These shared affinities will become opportunities. The more you find out, the more options you have, with these physical common interests, to spend time together engaged in these activities. Now, you may be thinking, "Going to restaurants won't necessarily solidify any bonds," and you're absolutely right. But look what happens here.

Every physical common interest that you guys share is a potential setting to spend time together. There's an immediate level of comfort because you're engaging in activities that both of you enjoy. You're already managing to strengthen the twine between your two hearts *just* from going out on these dates. This is why the good dater will purposely try to craft dating scenarios born out of common interests. It almost immediately eliminates the new-date jitters. With those pesky kinks out of the way, you guys can focus on spending time together finding deeper commonalities.

Through the course of being close together, you guys will begin to build bonds rooted in common interests that lie on a deeper level than that of the physical. You may notice, through conversation, while on a date that you two share common viewpoints on politics, religion, the death penalty . . . Who knows? You may even notice, over the course of time, a similarity in expressing intimacy, causing disgusting displays of public affection. Whatever the case may be, it is the comfortable setting provided by physical common interests that allows you the opportunity to explore each other and find those deeper, mentally fixed interests you may share.

The compounding of these types of shared interests helps in building that stairway from the Friendship phase to the D8able phase.

Common Interests as a Foundation

For those who still want to downplay the importance of common interests, ask yourself this: Has a fledgling relationship of yours ever learned to fly without some common interests as the rocket fuel? Were you ever able to get past the first meeting with someone you didn't have anything to talk about with? Probably not. No one willfully deals with someone they can't connect with unless all they want is sex. Even still, the mutual want for sex is a commonality. It is a superficial common interest in the earlier goings, but a common interest nonetheless. Even negative common interests, like you both hating puppies, or babies, or summer breezes, are a rapport-building opportunity.

As stated earlier, common interests are the foundation for the development of your relationship while in the Friendship phase. Don't get it wrong, common interests play an important role throughout your relationship, but they are most influential and important during the early stages of the Friendship phase. They comprise the core for your relationship's growth toward a deeper, more significant connection. Think of the way a tree grows and it'll better help you understand. The physical common interests described earlier are the roots. The more you have, the stronger the foundation, and the greater the opportunity for your connection to develop into a real force of nature—oak, if you will.

Engaging in activity based on the roots is what fosters the growth of common connection. In other words, the more time you spend together, the stronger the bond can become in regard to the physical commonalities. The trunk of the tree is representative of the strength of the bonds built from you guys actually going out and spending time together. You two can develop enjoyment in going out with each other.

During these excursions, you get to observe each other in real time. You discover more similarities, some that have nothing to do with a physical common interest. These would be the multitude of branches growing out from the trunk of the tree: those common interests, viewpoints, and positions that reside in the mental portions of who you two are. Your common interests, all types, along with other elements to be discussed shortly, work in unison to produce the lush, green, nourishing leaves of your relationship.

You're progressing closer to D8able status as the uncovering of more common interests takes place. The development of deep rapport, which is arguably the origin of love, is initiated through these means.

Below is the example of your "tree" of common interests:

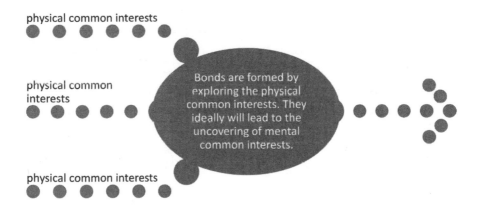

Okay, so it looks more like a freaky alien sperm cell than a tree, but it'll work for the purposes of explaining the tree idea. As you can see, the physical common interests all act as the roots for developing a strong rapport because they're the very first set of common interests that can be explored. These would be the initial dates you go on with your potential mate. The more physical common interests you have, the stronger the roots, or the more opportunities you have to spend time engaging in mutually enjoyable activities. From the roots comes the bond built from spending all that time on dates. The stronger this bond becomes, the greater the possibility for further exploration of mutual interests. However, the mutual interests you'll start to uncover will begin to be rooted in the mental interests you two have in common. The arrow represents the branches of mutual connection that lead you closer to the D8able phase.

Support System

Yes, your common interests are quite the tool for relationship fortification and growth. They will serve two purposes as your relationship continues to progress. They'll act as your safety net in regard to relationship building. Your common interests will also provide the inspiration for you to further explore your loved one, and for them to do the same.

We are optimists at heart. People may not readily admit this, but we secretly want things to go well. When we're lucky enough to meet someone whom we can picture calling our own, we can't help but imagine future scenarios with them as our costars. Our optimistic, forward-looking outlooks are the result of the positive mutual exploration we've been a part of.

Having common interests, and finding out about those similarities can be very alluring, even addictive. When you're having fun, what's the only thing that can top it? More fun, of course. If you're lucky enough to come across a person who seems to fit together with you like children's building blocks, you want to see just how many of those blocks you can add to this construction you call a relationship.

Finding out about mutual interests inspires you to want to discover more. More importantly, finding out you two have so much in common can brand you adventurous. Proactive couples will seek new adventures, trying to find more mutual interests they didn't previously know they had. This is actually one of the steps to keeping a relationship fresh in the future, the want to continue to push it forward, to help it continuously evolve. Continuing to build these particular bonds of common interests is probably the most fun and most natural of the tasks involved in developing and maintaining a strong union.

The other side of the common interests support system is the safety net. People would like to believe that they have everything in common with their new, bright, and shiny love interest. Over time they'll realize that this isn't quite the case. A major part of learning about your would-be significant other is uncovering the differences you have as well.

No two people are exactly alike, not even twins . . . And twins dating each other just sounds weird. But let's not digress. No two people involved with each other are going to have everything in common. Not only would this be extremely boring, it's just a virtual impossibility. Your experiences, goals, fears, needs, and wants are uniquely yours alone. Those elements that make up your love interest are equally as unique. You will definitely connect on a lot of mutual affinities, but you'll also have your fair share of differences.

When two relatively mature individuals encounter their respective differences with one another, they don't run. Instead, they rely on the multitude of similarities to more than balance out the differences. This is their safety net. It won't matter if you're a Yankees fan and he's into Boston. Clearly, one of you has terrible taste, but the issue won't stand a chance in damaging your union because of all the commonalities you possess. Despite their differences, two mature daters can always fall back on their similarities to strengthen the bonds of their union.

It should also be said that differences aren't even close to being a negative aspect of the relationship, unless you two make it that way. Remember a while back when we discussed how solid relationships are made? How this involves two whole people joining to make a greater whole? If not, go back and read it again. A whole person is a person for himself or herself, not for other people. With that being said, not only should you and your mate have differences, but it should be expected that these differences will arise.

You should want to have differences. Read it again: you should want to have differences. You two had lives before you met, and no one should be expected to totally change their life just because they're in a new relationship currently. Differences are a major indicator that you're dating a whole individual and not a half-person hoping you'll fill the voids in their life.

Differences are their own adventure. When your common-interests game is strong, you can treat differences as something to be explored as well. Why? Because, if you two happen to not enjoy the exploration of the differences, you have that mutual interest's safety net to fall back on. Who knows, you could be exposed to something you previously thought you didn't enjoy, only to find out that you actually do.

No Common Interests?

What happens when you have no common interests, or at least, your exploration doesn't generate new ones? Is it time to pack up your shit and leave? Some people do. So what would be the play here? This really depends on the people involved. It could very well be that you guys have reached your limits of compatibility. Or, you two can be stubborn. Stubborn is always fun. Find common interests. Be proactive and test-drive new adventures. Do things that neither of you thought you'd enjoy.

Remember, we're ever evolving, and so are our relationships. Things you may have hated at twenty-five may hold your interest at thirty-five. If you want to try to hold on to that relationship you've been working at, think outside of the box. There will be a lot of trial and error, but isn't that what life is anyway?

Building common interests from scratch can open a whole new door of understanding for who you are as an individual as well as the person you are in your relationship. Think of it as simultaneous self-discovery between you and your mate. You two could come out of this better than you went in. A little work, a fine-tune, a little attention to detail, and you could have the new relationship smell once more. So, how do you go about doing this?

One would think that the route to go with this would have to involve something neither of you have ever done. Find something both of you have sidestepped trying in the past, a mutual disinterest, if you will. It should preferably be of an exciting or thrilling nature. That way, even if you don't like it, you two will have the chance to bond on the basis of the excitement. If that fails, try, try, try again.

If you guys truly care for each other, and the only issue is a deficit in the common interest department, then a premature scrapping of the union may be a mistake. Push it until the wheels fall off.

Pros and Cons

There are always pros and cons in any situation. It is up to you to evaluate that situation in order to make the best decision for you. We briefly gave you an alternate route when facing the cons of not having any real common interests—the con, of course, being the fact that you don't have much of a foundation to build upon. Not having common interests early in the game can really shut the game down . . . if you let it. But if you focus on the pros, then you could work things out. Not having many early common interests then demands the two involved in the relationship to create their own common interests. People willing to do this show a rare dedication to a relationship that many other folks do not have.

Having a lot of common interests easily has its pros. The two involved, at least earlier in the dating game, can feel like the relationship is perfect, airtight, no need for improvement. But, as we all know, nothing is perfect and all things can be improved upon, especially relationships. So what can the con of having too much in common really be? It seems sort of silly that a con could actually exist for this situation, right? Having too much in common can be a bad thing?

Yes, it can! For one reason, and one reason only, having too much in common can be detrimental. Why? Because it promotes complacency. People make the mistake of getting lazy when they feel as if they have nothing to work toward. You see it at the job. You see it with professional athletes who have the talent but no drive to improve on that talent. And you definitely can see it in relationships.

Things go stale when you don't work to keep them fresh. Assuming that your relationship will stand the test of time based on what you have right now is a mistake. If we're always growing and changing, then so will the relationships we are a part of. Because of this, it behooves us to continue to look for those common interests to keep the bond strong.

Believing in the perfection of a union also breeds the dysfunctional idea that you have no differences between you and your mate. This is also ludicrous. Unless you're dating your clone, everyone has some differences. The lack of evaluating these differences and of fostering these differences can lead to one or both people involved feeling slighted. Differences, when approached correctly, can actually add to the stability of a relationship. To ignore them is to ignore an opportunity to fortify your union.

Lastly, the most detrimental part of assuming that your union is perfect is the mistake of forgetting what you did to originally catch your mate. This has been said before, but needs to be reiterated. Common interests don't mean shit if you're not making the best of them. They don't mean a damn thing if you're not looking for new ones.

If you and your significant other have ceased mutually exploring one another, your relationship will reach a level of comfort that can actually eat away at it from the inside. Have you ever heard of the term metabolic syndrome? Fitness professionals use this term to describe the systematic breakdown in your bodily functions because of lack of activity.

The same goes for your relationship. If you allow your relationship to sit on the shelf for forty hours a week, it'll systematically begin to crumble as well. If you don't want future complications that'll eventually lead to severe dysfunction, do yourself a favor and work on keeping your relationship active.

Preservation

For good relationships, well, keeping the relationship in the "good" category is not an easy task. Relationships are hard work, and they should be. They need to be worked at constantly. As stated earlier, common interests play an important role in preserving relationships in the form of a safety net. When your relationship hits a rough patch, and it probably will at some point, that safety net of common interests, along with the caring and mutual respect you two have for one another can be the salvation of your union.

The importance of being selfless in a relationship has already been stated multiple times throughout this manual. Realizing that your mate's needs and wants should take precedence over your own can really help with the preservation of your coupling. Add the passion for finding new common interests to build upon the bonds you've already developed, and you're doing a solid job fortifying your union when negativity comes your way.

When you guys argue, you both can step back and remember those commonalities. You can both remember not to be selfish. You can both remember to give precedence to each other's needs. When external negativity comes your way, again, having this mind-set and that safety net of mutual interests can be quite the bunker. Having each other's backs, and knowing the feeling is mutual, is very powerful. Common interests and caring can be that buffer to weather multiple storms.

CHAPTER 7

DATING PREJUDICE OR PREFERENCE

RESPECT, APPRECIATION, REASONABLE EXPECTATIONS

We've previously touched on the elements involved in choosing a mate. Most are rooted in personal preference. Some are rooted in the influence of outside sources. We discussed, in length, the way our brains work when deciding on the aspects a person has that we perceive to be crucial qualities. Without those qualities, many times we deem the person "un-D8able."

The laundry list, as we so affectionately named it, is the entire list of qualities you or your love interest has created that outlines what you would want in a mate . . . respectively. If you can recall, these lists are also heavily decided by the superficial portions of our brains, meaning that some of the qualities we *think* we need really have no substance behind them. We've also spent a lot of time discussing an innovative way to go about separating the necessary qualities from the "Icing on the Cake" qualities.

We've also discussed the idea of having appreciation and reasonable expectations for the person you decide to date. All of these discussions are to help get you better equipped for the dating world by getting you out of your own way. They are an attempt to get you to look at your dating life in an objective manner, maybe even to unlock the mental shackles you may have that are causing you to repeat the same mistakes time and again.

With that being said, many of the choices you make come down to personal preference. But what if, just if, some of those preferences you have are rooted in prejudiced behavior? Would you be willing to listen to reason? If so, read on. If not, run the risk of seriously crippling your chances in the dating world . . .

To Prejudge

Developing an opinion on something or someone without actually having any reason to is considered prejudiced activity. When people think of prejudiced activity they usually think of actions born out of negative preconceived notions. Prejudiced activity can also be actions originating from positive preconceived notions as well. Either way, setting a plan of action into play based on either type of prejudice is never a good move. You can severely cripple your ability to maneuver in the social world. Some of these prejudiced ideas can be embedded so deeply into the way you think, speak, and act that you don't even realize they're there. Like tiny little parasites, they can feed on your ability to make the best decision for yourself based on an idea that carries little to no weight in critical thinking.

Let's revisit superficial thinking for a second, just to make a point. Do you remember what we defined as superficial action in the dating game? We defined it as action based solely on what was seen. Superficiality is what initially attracts us to a potential mate . . . remember? It is, on some level, a necessity because it aids in creating preference (check out the chapter "The Superficial Gay: Intimacy"). The majority of the superficial thought process is based on visual stimulation to fuel initial attraction. At least superficial thought comes from actually seeing something, or from direct interaction with someone. Prejudiced ideas can originate from having little experience to none at all with the object of prejudgment. This does not mean, however, that prejudiced ideas originate out of thin air.

So, where do these ideas come from? What makes someone wake up one day and totally exclude someone else based on absolutely nothing? What influences are involved in the prejudiced ideas that result in one person excluding another based on grounds as weighty as air? We are often the products of our respective environments. This includes the negative elements of our character we develop as well.

One could argue that because none of us are born with any sort of prejudice, it's one of those nasty habits we learn from others . . . sort of like robbing old ladies, or farting in a crowded elevator. Dating prejudice is a strong example of this, a crappy habit learned from a faulty outside source. Similar to those dating laundry lists we've come to love, our prejudices need to be cast aside to make way for a new, more progressive way of thinking.

Weak Foundation

Prejudices of any kind are built upon a weak foundation constructed from little truth, ignorant hearsay, and just plain stupidity. Dating prejudices are constructed of the same shoddy material. Society as a whole, friends, and family all play the part in perpetuating stereotypes of certain people, furthering unfounded prejudices. The person who adheres to such lunacy is the person who stands to pigeonhole himself of herself in the dating game.

The prejudgment that exists is the direct result of these negatively concocted categorizations. Types of media may portray a certain group in a certain light. Then, people on an individual level are exposed to these stereotypes. Many of these people begin to believe and perpetuate these falsehoods about groups that they themselves either don't even belong to or have had no real dealings with. What's worse is the fact that people within the group being targeted for negative stereotypes, or stereotypes in general, for that matter, can begin to believe or even perpetuate those same stereotypes. This all adds to the prejudices floating around out there. There is a difference between perception and realness. There is a difference between fact and someone's opinion based on little-to-no knowledge. Prejudices are rooted in flawed, uneducated perception and fed by the opinions of the ignorant and unknowing.

There is a common theme amongst people who don't do well in the chess game we all know as dating and relationships. That theme is the want to be lazy on some level, the want for others to think for them. These types of people don't want to put in the work to do real self-exploration or truly evaluate potential mates. Believe me, it's much easier to create a laundry list of qualities for the perfect mate, and continue to fail, than it is to take ownership over your personal faults and train yourself to be a better dater. It's much easier to be what society says you should be to fit in than it is to figure out who you truly are in the world. It is much easier to take the advice of others (including the truly ignorant jargon) than it is to think critically and figure out the best way to go about doing things on your own. It is far easier to believe in stereotypes, alienate a whole group of people for unfounded reasons, and live by prejudices than it is to take each person you meet as an individual.

This way of thinking not only makes you look like an idiot, but it severely diminishes the chances you'll meet someone worthwhile as well. Remember when we addressed overlooking people because they lacked a few qualities on our respective laundry lists? We outlined exactly how you could run the risk of missing out on someone great because they don't fit the perfect description of what you want. Rejecting groups of people based on stereotype and prejudice is even worse because you're not even giving yourself a chance to see what qualities a person has due to a predetermined idea of the type of person they are . . . What if you end up turning down a potential soul mate because you're prejudiced against older folks, or shorter people, or someone from a different region than your own. It seems silly when you're reading it, but many people subscribe to this very practice.

When you sit back and think about it, where do prejudices and stereotypes get their strength and longevity? This ignorance thrives on, well, people *wanting* to be ignorant. The moment you decide that this isn't the way you want to be is the moment you can remove this self-made hurdle out of your relationship race.

Perception, Not Truth

Somebody somewhere had something happen on a date with a certain person. Good or bad, this particular scenario was somehow blown out of proportion. More people found out about this, and eventually, *all* people similar to that certain person got stuck with the same label. Stereotype. Enough people listening to said stereotype make judgments about those certain people, even if personally, these people have never had any interaction whatsoever with said stereotyped certain people. Prejudice.

You can pretend that you've never been exposed to this behavior. You'd be lying only to yourself. If you've ever heard any verbiage describing an entire group of people a certain way, such as "all of them" or "those people," then you've been privy to a prejudice born out of a stereotype. If you've ever made a decision concerning someone based on this type of "information," then you have just perpetuated that stereotype.

It is a true poison in the dating world. Just think of how many people have overlooked good candidates because of their adherence to silly rumors and hearsay. Think of the narrow road that people who adhere to stereotypes have chosen to travel. They're willfully cutting off a multitude of options. They are limiting their chances of happiness, as if the erroneously constructed laundry list of qualities wasn't stifling enough.

Have you ever listened to someone's reasons for staying away from an entire group of people? The reasons never seem to make all that much sense. Even more ridiculous are the motives people have to date *only* a certain group. Surely you've heard something similar to "I don't date short men because their dicks are tiny." Or maybe "I date only white girls because they know how to treat you better than everyone else."

Seriously? Just because he's five feet four inches doesn't necessarily mean he's packing a twenty-two, and just because she's white doesn't mean she's genetically predisposed to being a gentler, kinder mate. One, two, or even a handful of negative experiences (or good ones, for that matter) with people of a similar background or makeup does not make you the expert on all of them. You've just been the unlucky soul who happens to stumble upon baby penis after baby penis. There are just as many short guys with decent-sized members as there are men who got the short end of the stick. There are just as many mean and manipulative women as there are angels who'll have your back during the tough times. A person's height, weight, religion, hotness level, dick size, race, age (as long as they're a legal adult), hand size, hairstyle, shoe color, eye color, dog's name, or mother's birth city will not determine the type of person they are. Period.

The only thing prejudice accomplishes is to show what type of numbskull you can be in the dating world. You're doing nothing more than hurting yourself and your chance to find someone worthwhile.

Let's look at something like ageism, for example. For those of you who don't know what this is, ageism is the discrimination of someone based on their age. They are often prejudged and stereotyped because of how old, and even sometimes how young, they are. In the dating and relationship game, less worth is placed on someone who may be too old or too young. Younger adults can be falsely viewed as inexperienced or immature. Older people can be viewed as impotent and less sexual because of their advanced age.

Clearly, there are a lot more prejudices linked to something like ageism, but you can see from the examples some of the hurdles people may have to face when trying to connect intimately with others. Socially acceptable, prejudiced thought processes such as these can limit the ability for people to find love. This is because people are expected to be grouped with what society deems to be their own kind. We shouldn't even have terms like "May–December" relationships (which allude to an older person dating a younger one), but they exist because we as a society feel the need to categorize everything.

We see these terms everywhere. Gay relationships. Lesbian relationships. Interracial relationships. Polyamorous relationships. Whatever happened to just . . . relationships, of an intimate nature? A union between two people who care for one another regardless. These terms reveal, in a lot of ways, that society isn't truly accepting of many scenarios, just recognizably tolerant. Newsflash, people: Love is love no matter what classification you want to give it. Love is love.

And here we go as a people . . . adhering . . . to stereotypes and prejudices about others and in some cases even ourselves.

Predetermined Dating

A prejudice is still a prejudice regardless of whether or not the particular idea connotes negativity. The negative ideas about a person or group serve as a falsified, trumped-up warning. They urge you to stay away at all costs. Remember the section on expectations and reasonable expectations? It focused on teaching you how to determine if you're being reasonable within the relationships you engage in. Well, reasonable expectations also play a part in prejudice, on both sides of the same coin.

On one hand, is it a reasonable expectation to believe that everyone of a certain group is negative, or should be avoided when seeking a mate? No, of course not. It is impossible to know, much less believe, that all folks of a certain group act the same way. It's good to keep your guard up, but that goes for all people, not a select group or groups. Don't make the mistake of building a wall so high that you miss out on a good person because of a silly misconception about that person.

People aren't items to be purchased at a discount warehouse. You can't find good-natured daters on aisle one. Big-dicked people aren't on aisle seven. In a lot of ways, dating can be trial and error. You have to take everyone individually as you cross each other's path. There's no real way to know whom you're getting in the initial stages of the dating game. No predetermined ideas about any group can serve as a GPS to navigate you through the dating streets.

On the other side of the same coin are those prejudices that seem to suggest the positivity of certain groups. A prejudice rooted in positive stereotypes is still growing out of a stereotype. When you blindly follow a prejudice, even one that seems to promote good aspects of a group of people, you're still running into the woods blindly. In some ways, believing positive stereotypes about a certain group of people can harm you more than isolating yourself from other groups.

When you believe in the overarching righteousness of a particular group, you'll blindly chase after it. Your guard will be all the way down. Couple this with having "type" issues and you can begin to see the danger involved. Remember, we have defined your type as the person possessing a conglomerate of qualities and characteristics that you're attracted to. Having a type means that you've gone after this particular kind of person multiple times without success . . . which in essence means that your type really isn't your type at all. Your type is sort of the open flame and you're the blinded moth circling it in danger of burning up.

Now, let's examine this a bit further, shall we? You've pigeonholed yourself by staying away from certain groups based on prejudice rooted in negative stereotypes. You have a laundry list of qualities you chase after in hopes of securing the perfect mate. You have a "type" you've been chasing for quite a while now that seems to leave you empty and heartbroken over and over again, meaning they couldn't possibly or truly be your type. To top it all off, you run blindly toward a particular group of people because of some silly prejudice rooted in so-called positive stereotypes. Your brain has been hoodwinked and your heart is running in circles in its cage. You've created a road so narrow, it's a wonder you've managed to meet anyone at all. You may as well answer that ad selling unicorns in your local newspaper. Is it no wonder that so many people seem so utterly lost when it comes to securing a mate?

No group of people is totally homogenous. No one, regardless of stereotype, can truly be expected to fulfill all of your needs.

Unfair Expectations

When you go after someone based on a stereotype, you're not only blindly believing in something with no substance, you're placing unfair expectations on the object of your affections. Take a look at this scenario:

You have come to believe that the only group of people worthy of dating is white men. You've heard that all white men treat their mates like royalty. All white men are financially stable. All white men are absolutely perfect in relationships. Maybe you've learned this from your mother and father, maybe you've been brainwashed by the media's negative portrayal of other guys. It doesn't matter how this ideology came about in your brain, all that matters is that it exists. Based on what you *think* you know, you've decided to go out only with white guys under the pretense that they'll fit the aforementioned description. Add your laundry list to the mix, and just for good measure, let's put your "type" qualifications in there as well. You now have this concrete image in your head of the type of guy you're going to go after.

Not only have you narrowed your search by excluding all others, but your unreal expectations of white guys will most likely leave you dissatisfied with the guys you do come across. Here's the real mindfuck: you've conditioned yourself to go after only this mythical, unicorn-like white guy. Your laundry list of qualities and your so-called type will clearly lead you to candidates, but the mountain-high, insurmountable standards you have will more than likely leave you disappointed time and time again. People will continue to come up short as you look for that mate, that white guy who's perfect in every way.

But, it's embedded in your brain. So you keep going, you keep searching for this perfect white guy. You overstep everyone else, some bad and some very good candidates, all because they don't fit into this image of whom you want. You've allowed a silly stereotype to seriously retard your critical thinking in hopes of landing that perfect knight in shining armor, the white guy . . .

It sounds silly when you read it, but how many people do you know who have said something like this? "I date only white guys because . . ." "I go out only with black dudes because . . ." "Oh no, I'd never go out with a . . ." It is absolute and utter ridiculousness.

Oh, we're not done yet. You've decided to drown yourself in a sea of white men. Fair enough. But, you've begun to notice that none of these guys is that perfect mate. They're not turning out to be the men your momma said they'd be. Your clouded brain can't figure out why no one is perfect. Some get closer than others, but none of the white men you've met have been exactly what you wanted.

Instead of realizing that there are no perfect mates (regardless of a shitty stereotype suggesting otherwise), you begin to internalize the issue. You believe you're the problem and that's why your perfect white man hasn't swept you off of your feet and taken you off into the sunset . . .

Sounds like a snowball argument, right? This story doesn't seem all that believable? Think again, because it happens quite often. People get so caught up in the wrong things about someone, like their skin color, height, and so on, that they can totally overlook the great things those people have to offer.

And what about those guys? What about those white guys you met who didn't reach the bar? They were faced with unreal, unfair expectations. Sure, some of them were probably douchebags, as douchebags do come in all shapes, sizes, colors, and creeds. But, you'd lose a wager if you assumed that all of them were bad people. Because of your unreal expectations, you probably ran off some pretty good guys.

This may seem like an extreme case, but we've all had a friend or even been that person who alienates good folks because they come up short on a few characteristics.

Undeserved Credit

So-called positive stereotypes and prejudices can actually aid in giving people passes they don't deserve. If you're indoctrinated into believing that one group of people surpasses another, in any social realm including dating, then you may be overlooking the universal constant we all have. Flaws. It is an inescapable truth: we are all flawed. People make mistakes and this fact is a huge part of being human.

No matter who you are, and where you come from, you have the capacity to be selfless or selfish. You have the capacity to do right and wrong, to be a nice person or an utter asshole. The problem with some positive stereotypes is that they can paint the picture that certain groups are above this particularly general human trait of imperfection. The person who subscribes to such prejudice can actually cloud their own brain and not think clearly when dealing with those folks. Red flags are red flags for a reason, but the delusional can often ignore them.

Take, for instance, the example illustrated earlier. One person "dates only" a particular type of person because they have come to believe that people only from this particular subset of the population are worthy of dating. This is an actual affirmation, in the dater's mind, that this specific group is better . . . for whatever reason. Because of this, the dater has already put himself or herself in a lower position, especially if the dater doesn't also fit into that subset of people. Get it?

In other words, say you date only black men, for whatever reason, but you yourself aren't black. Your reasons for dating black men are rooted in a so-called positive stereotype. You're subconsciously admitting to yourself that you hold black men higher on the dating totem pole than all other people, including yourself. You're also putting yourself in a lower position, treating this particular group of people as something to be attained, instead of realizing that we are all on the same level. None of us is perfect. None of us deserves to start with a shiny gold medal before the dating race has even begun.

Whatever their motivations, people with this thought process—this mind-set to either discredit whole groups or wholeheartedly accept others—are seriously missing the point of having an analytical brain that can readily categorize people based on substance and quantifiable behavior. They don't have to rely on the words of an ignorant influence. Hell, they themselves don't have to be ignorant. All it takes is the want to truly succeed in life, or for the purposes of this manual, the want to succeed in the art of dating and relationships specifically.

Missing Out

It was touched on earlier but definitely needs to be revisited. Prejudice's main function is to make you miss out on other people. It's as simple as that. The idea of making a judgment call on anyone before actually dealing with that person is ridiculous. Being prejudiced means being socially lazy. Anyone can tell you the dating game is not a game for the lazy. Those who opt for that socially and mentally lazy existence will not get very far in the game.

With all things, you need to ask yourself how bad you want it. Relationships are no different. Even after reading this manual from cover to cover, even after attending every D8able LLC workshop, if you don't go out and work, you won't get what you want. Those who truly want the chance to succeed in dating, relationships, and love can't afford to waste their time believing in such hogwash as stereotypes. They don't have the luxury (if you can call ignorance a luxury) of being prejudiced against people. This manual has preached, over and over again, that the most important part of dating is self and self-exploration. A part of self-exploration is evaluating how you interact with others on a social level. Well, just how the hell do you plan on interacting with anyone if you're allowing stereotypes and prejudice to build a wall around you?

The mate you need is out there, so don't make it harder than it already is to find them.

Individually Speaking . . .

Everyone is unique. We are the sum of our experiences. We are the passions and goals that drive us. Our respective sexual preferences, eye color, hair color, ethnic background, height, weight, and even credit score all add to our respective uniqueness. Identical twins even have things that separate them. The way we grew up, the parents we have, and everything we've been through up to three . . . two . . . one . . . second ago help define who we are as individuals. With that being said, you need to learn to take everyone—everyone—on an individual basis.

When it comes to dating, every person you meet will be a brand-new experience. It will behoove you to leave your previous experiences on the shelf. Give this new person a chance to separate himself or herself from the pack. It is okay to be cautious based on previous experiences; it is not okay to let previous experiences govern how you treat new people. Use the things you've learned about yourself to help guide you with this new person. Do not use some silly prejudice to cancel people out of the game before they even get the chance to play.

You'll have much more variety, much more fun, and a greater chance of meeting your mate if you approach dating with a more liberal view.

CHAPTER 8

DATING APPS, OR THE MORE THINGS CHANGE

COMMON INTERESTS, LISTENING, REASONABLE EXPECTATIONS, RISK, VULNERABILITY

We would like to think things change, progress for the better. Technology exists for one reason, and that's to make our lives easier, some would argue, and more efficient. There is no mistaking the fact that many of those technological advancements we have today do indeed make life a lot more manageable. Planes, trains, and automobiles are clearly some of the more substantial advancements of our age. Could you imagine going cross-country on a friggin' stagecoach? And what about all of the medical advancements out there? Three hundred or four hundred years ago, the common cold could wipe out a decent percentage of the population. Oh, and the Internet in general. Looking things up has never been so easy. Or would you rather go back to the Dewey Decimal System at the libraries? And let's not forget the advancements in hair plugs and toupees . . . giving balding men confidence all over the world, one shiny head at a time.

Then there are the dating applications.

The great-great-grandfather of the modern-day dating application first showed up around 1700. It was known as a matrimonial service where the ads were posted in the local newspaper. Videodating made its appearance in the 1980s. The first actual online dating site went live in 1995. It's safe to say that some form of alternative dating has existed before you even had an interest in dating and relationships. The real question is, has the introduction of alternative dating legitimately changed the face of dating?

Well, yes and no . . .

Dating applications have introduced some very innovative components to the dating world as a whole. A person's chances to meet other people have exponentially grown, at least in the sense of how widespread their reach is. Does expanding one's reach actually improve one's batting average? Does flirting online guarantee meeting the person of your dreams? Many people seem to think so. But, the more things seem to change, the more they can actually mirror the past. As a matter of fact, the traditional aspects of dating that have changed because of the advent of online dating applications arguably have not changed for the better.

Do dating applications create a more inviting, more user-friendly environment for dating and relationships?

Pro Applications

With so many dating applications out there, and so many people plugged in, the applications must bring a ton of never-before-seen innovation to the dating arena, right? Well, maybe not as much as you think, but the dating applications are useful in a handful of areas.

As stated earlier, dating applications have introduced some very innovative components to the dating world as a whole. In an attempt to separate one dating application from another, the creators of these respective apps add features to their apps to make them slightly different from the pack. There's an app out there that makes you answer 1,001 questions before you can upload a photo. It then tries to match you with other folks based on your answers to these questions and your location. The questions are rather silly but are a feeble attempt at personality matching . . . something a matchmaker will always be better suited for than an algorithm in a buggy dating app can ever be.

There's a dating application out there that tries to organize events based on your location. Mass text messages are sent out to people in your area through the app. Again, the hands-on assistance and experience of an actual event organizer and dating consultant beat out a text-message bomb via a dating app with ease.

Then there are the apps that stick to being simple. All they do is tug at your need for initial superficiality and appease that urge. You simply swipe one way if you like someone, swipe the opposite way if you don't. Very simple. Very simple and innovative, yet extremely empty in terms of an overall date-changing experience.

The most useful advancement, by far, that dating applications have brought to the dating game is the expansion of a dater's reach. Because all applications use the Internet as their medium, users have the opportunity to be exposed to other online daters virtually anywhere, though most applications have a discovery range of about fifty miles max. This means, in layman speak, that the user searches on these applications will pull the info for online daters up to about a fifty-mile radius from your current location. Now that most applications have a smartphone version of the application, you can online-date on the go . . . instead of, ummm, meeting someone in the real world, while you're on the go.

The other pro to online dating is the sea of profiles right at your fingertips. You can browse thousands of potential dates' profiles, including their bios, with nothing more than the click of a button, or a swipe . . . it depends on the particular app you use, but you get the picture. Online dating does open your doors to people you may have never met otherwise. Users can basically decide whom to pursue from this menu of eligible potential dates . . . and by pursue, we mean message incessantly until they block you for online stalker-ish activity.

And that's about it. Surely, the creators of these apps would argue on behalf of the other so-called dating advancements. But if you look at everything objectively, a wider range of possible people to interact with and information about these possible meet-ups are pretty much the extent of online dating advancement . . . Oh, and maybe something about personality matching.

But how do these things improve your standing in the dating world?

Dating Con

Dating applications bring a few new things to the table—namely, a wider reach and much more information in the preliminary stages in regard to the person or people you're interested in meeting. While those two advancements can be helpful (can be, but not necessarily), there is much to consider as far as the negative elements that online dating also introduces . . . or, reinvents. To say that online dating brings a host of new negativity to the dating game would be false. Honestly, online dating doesn't bring anything newly negative to the table. It does, however, amplify or enhance a lot, if not all, of the negativity that already exists.

What is technology if not the tool to make things in life more accessible, easy, and efficient? This includes being an asshole. Think the bionic-douchebag, Jerk-Off 2.0, and you'll begin to see where we're going with this. Dating applications, in a lot of ways, have made it easier for the scum of the dating world to survive—no, thrive . . . As a matter of fact, one could argue that online dating has enabled those who would otherwise be considered decent yet awkward people the chance to get into the dating world. While this isn't necessarily a bad thing, if absolute power can corrupt absolutely, what is a dating site that exposes an otherwise overlooked person to thousands of potential dates going to do? The worst-case scenario is the transformation of said person into an uber-asshole.

Yes, ladies and gentleman, just like technology can make it easier to clean your house, pay your bills, or shop, so can it enable jerks, assholes, and players to do what they do, on a grander scale, with the help of cyber-smoke and digital mirrors. With every new innovation a dating app releases to the public, a new way is found to exploit that innovation, to use it for the forces of evil . . . Well, maybe not evil. There are no megalomaniacal super-villains waiting to conquer the planet via a dating website. But, there are the jerks who get off on playing cyber-dating games through online mediums.

Some Drawbacks

As with other types of technology, there are certain drawbacks that can reveal themselves with dating apps. The nature of a dating app is such that it promotes a so-called easier way to date. This isn't true, and we'll discuss this later. These apps don't promote dating ease. They promote dating laziness. A lazy dater isn't a good one. Have you ever heard the saying "Anything worth having is worth working for"? Well, at least in the realm of dating, this is absolutely true.

Dating is work, and finding the right person can be a real journey of self-discovery. Don't believe that? Then go back and reread this entire manual. A major part of the joy created from dating is the mutual self-discovery you go through with your potential love interest. A lot of that discovery is taken away from you through the use of dating apps.

Dating applications also have the tendency to build a false sense of arrogance in their users. If you're already arrogant, then so be it. But, what does a person who's never had any real attention crave the most? Exactly. Even the person who lacks attention gets it in the real world. They simply may not notice the amount of attention because it's spread out over the course of a time frame.

When you wake up, log on to your favorite dating site, and see fifty-nine unread messages from potential suitors, it can do a number on your self-confidence. All of a sudden, you're the queen of the cyber-dating world. Why is this new cyber-self-confidence rooted in fallacy? Because . . . true self-confidence is constructed through real self-exploration, through the fostering of the true you, not through the attention of a bunch of digital suitors who don't even know the real you.

Dating online also promotes the use of your "laundry lists" and the search for your "types." You can fine-tune your search to find people with all of the characteristics you think you need to have the perfect mate—at least, their profiles *say* they are your perfect match. As you probably remember, your laundry list of qualities and your "type" are more often than not some of the bigger hurdles you have to get over to be a better dater. Laundry lists promote the idea of the perfect mate, and your type is that collection of qualities you're attracted to . . . But it doesn't quite work out for you, hence the reason you have a type and not a mate with all those qualities.

Online Booty-Shopping

In a lot of ways, this is exactly what online dating can be: online shopping for booty. It's just a matter of finding the profile you like, placing your bid (a clever message), and waiting for a response. There's no real skill involved. There's no learning curve. You don't have to be comfortable enough with yourself to approach that hot guy, because you're not approaching him. You're checking out photos of him, reading his ingredients, clicking a few buttons, and crossing your fingers for a reply.

Rhetorical questions: What are players usually highly skilled at? Getting some ass? Are players excellent in the art of seduction? What are players really good at? People of leisure, vampires, or players, as they're more commonly known, are excellent in the skill of gathering information and then using that information for personal gain. A player can take what they know about you, find a way to fill any voids you may have, gain your trust, and then get what they want out of you . . . whatever that may be. It all starts with the gathering of information.

Online dating has made it just that much easier to get said information. Even before Don Juan has typed two characters to you, he can pull up your profile and begin to pull out what he deems as important personal information he needs to connect with you. If his online presence is attractive enough, someone will take the bait, and thus begins the "asshole I met online" tale. Half of his mission was handed to him in a nice, bright, dating profile.

What's worse is the number of wannabe lotharios and lotharias floating around on Internet dating sites. They can't muster up the courage in the real world to go after anyone, but in front of their respective computer screens and smartphones, these folks turn into ice-cold word pimps. By uploading a few decent-looking pics taken from flattering angles, and equipping themselves with a decent thesaurus, they can say all the right shit to have people swarming like flies.

Dating sites are enabling the socially underdeveloped to run right alongside the players, mucking up the digital waters. One of the biggest drawbacks to the online dating world is in fact how foggy that world can be. In an online world, where everyone can get attention and everyone can pretend to be whoever they please, separating the real from the fake can be a daunting task for the serious dater.

Den of Liars and Thieves

Once thought of as the dating haven saving people from the real world, online dating is becoming more clear to people now. It isn't the digital savior. It's not the benevolent younger prince waiting to assume the throne of dating and relationships from its older, more corrupt brother. Online dating is the spitting mirror image of its real-world counterpart. Why? Because the same people you'd meet in the real world are logging on now. You've got the serious daters. You know, the folks who really want a relationship. You've got the grown children who don't know what they want. Then you have the leeches and bottom-feeders, the same selfish twits from the real world who are back in digital form.

One could make the argument that digital dating makes it easier for wolves to slip into their sheep uniforms. People can be whoever they want to be online. There's no real way to check. You can choose the name you want. You can choose the stats you want: how much money you make, your job, your height, the list goes on and on. You don't even have to use your own picture. The online dating world has made it easier for social predators to dig in deep and wait for their prey.

Bottom-Feeders

Better known as catfish, these particularly interesting people believe wholeheartedly in the phrase "Imitation is the greatest form of flattery." For those of you who've never heard of or experienced the beautifully disgusting spectacle that is the catfish, dig this: a catfish, in online dating terms, is a person who pretends to be another person. This doesn't mean they just change their name or tweak their online stats. No, catfish actually pose as other real people. This needs to be reiterated. Catfish pretend to be other actual living and breathing people.

They steal other people's identities. Maybe they snatch someone's photos from other social media outlets. They then construct a fake online persona that has nothing to do with who they really are. Then they go out for a digital hunt. They snare unsuspecting people looking for love online. They keep the charade going as long as possible, sometimes coaxing their victim to fall in love. All of this happens, of course, without the two people actually ever meeting . . .

They can't meet. They can never meet. The game would be over then. The catfish prefers to stay safely in front of their computer or smartphone, setting cyber-snare traps, emotionally devouring their prey from a safe distance.

The More They Stay the Same

What have we really learned from dating applications? Online dating is not some evolved form of dating. The digital cat-and-mouse game is almost exactly like the real world. You still have the exact elements that real-world social interaction has to offer. You have genuine folks out there, trying to meet someone, wading through the bullshit hoping to find a rose. You have the players, the dishonest people, and those who don't know what they want.

The social chess match still moves along, unchanged. People are still trying to figure out where they fit in the world. The advent of online dating didn't mean the elimination of the hurdles you face when attempting to meet your future significant other. The introduction of online dating didn't necessarily introduce new hurdles, it simply set up the same hurdles in different ways. There may be even more hurdles because of this new dating realm, but the type of obstacle remains the same.

Online dating is simply a scene you recognize, painted with a different tool set on a different medium. There isn't much to gain from online dating that you can't get in real-world interaction. The negativity produced from online dating mirrors that of the real-world negativities in dating. You stand to remain in almost the exact same place you started in regard to your journey through the dating world.

The scariest aspects of online dating are some people's overly positive reactions to it. People, who normally keep up a substantial emotional wall in the real world, can succumb to this false sense of safety in an online dating arena. They make a rather flawed assumption in thinking that the players and the low-lives somehow didn't receive the memo about the inception of online dating. No, no, no, no, no. Ask yourself this question: What is the universal constant amongst game players, low-lives, and hustlers?

They like cheating.

They like figuring out how to get something for little-to-no real work. They like figuring out how to manipulate a situation so it yields the best outcome for them, regardless of whom they may burn . . . Online dating sounds like just the place for people of this nature to dwell. They can easily disguise their true intentions with a few well-placed words. They can even hide what they look like if they see fit to do so. Let's not forget the real allure. Most people freely post the very information a user-type needs in order to attempt manipulation for personal gain.

Look at some of the personal shit you're asked to talk about on your profile. You're basically handing the players keys and combinations to the vault. Yes, no statistics have been compiled, but it's not absurd to assume that there could actually be a higher concentration of douchebags, dickheads, and downright despicable dog-minded motherfuckers online than those whom you'd run into on the streets on a periodic basis.

You won't be more educated in terms of dating dos and don'ts. You won't really have a better understanding of yourself either. Even though they're online, dating applications aren't Internet search engines geared to teach you how to understand the cat-and-mouse game any better. Actually, one could argue that the lack of social interaction because of online dating tools could in fact stunt your social growth.

No sir, no ma'am—true learning of self and your place in the world can happen only in the real world. The rest is just theory.

When the Pros Are Cons

We've discussed the advancements and the drawbacks that online dating has to offer. We've looked at the positive and negative aspects, on the whole, that they've introduced to the world. Overall, dating online brings similar obstacles that organic dating can bring. Either route you take, you're bound to hit a few potholes, have a few hiccups. That's life. That's the way things tend to go. Online dating mirrors its older brother in that respect. If you're one of those people who truly possesses self-understanding, dipping into the online dating world will seem a lot like running through the obstacle course of organic, real-world dating.

Those of us out there who haven't learned about self-exploration aren't in the same boat. If you haven't learned who you truly are, then walking the digital dating road won't get you any further than pounding the organic-dating pavement. Remember, everything starts with the self. Without the understanding of you, the real you, the road really makes no difference. This is something that dating apps can't teach you. It takes real work to learn the real you. People would like to believe they can skip this step, but there is no substitute for self-exploration and self-improvement. It doesn't matter how new and shiny the car is, if you're not trained to drive it, you're going to smash it up on the side of the road.

A better comparison would be to describe it like this . . .

Real-world dating is like playing the basketball game of your life. You feel the hardwood pressing against the soles of your shoes. You can smell the sweat and hear the aggression of the other players in the game. You feel the thrill of making a basket. All the while, you've learned a little bit more about yourself, about how you like to play the game.

Online dating is like playing the best basketball simulation of your life, on a next-gen gaming console. You can really dive into the world. The realism is so close to authentic that you can see the sweat on the computer-generated player's brow. You can pull off some dazzling moves on the screen, but what have you learned about yourself? Will you be able to make those dazzling moves on a real court? Online dating is not a hands-on learning experience. People don't want it to be, even though so many of us need that hands-on learning of self. Eventually, you'll have to meet this person you're courting in the real world, right? No number of emoticons, emojis, smiling faces, and cute little 140-characters-or-less messages can cover up a lack of self-understanding.

Or . . . you could compare real-world dating and online dating to running outside or on a treadmill, respectively . . .

So back to it. Online dating can shield you from a lot of social crap. But, in shielding you, online dating can also hinder your growth and progress in the social world. A lot of the steps you take when meeting and courting a potential mate are either lost or damn-near eliminated when utilizing the dating apps. Remember the journey we take from Bust-Down single to D8able duo? The dating apps neutralize some of the steps, which arguably can harm relationships in the long run.

The whole courting process is an opportunity. It's an opportunity to learn about your new love interest. It's an opportunity to learn about yourself, and it's the opportunity to learn whether or not you two have a shot at something substantial in the future. It's also a cat-and-mouse game that can be a hell of a lot of fun. But, when most dating apps provide a lot of the information up front that you'd normally discover over the course of time during the dating process, you lose a bit of the mystery. You lose the opportunity to explore. It's like knowing what you're getting for Christmas on December 24. Some of those dating profiles are so detailed that you can find out a guy's blood type before you have a clue what he sounds like.

Where's the Spark?

Dating apps can also throw off initial attraction. You do remember how preliminary attraction takes place, don't you? The spark. That instantaneous moment when you know, at the least, that you'd want to bed the object of your current, immediate affections. In the real world, you're eye-fucking a real person. Online, you're looking at images of someone . . . that may or may not be enhanced. In a worst-case scenario, they may not even be the real images of the person you're thinking about messaging.

Being attracted to an image doesn't give you that same *pow!* moment. Plus, you have to message the person on the other side of the image. You can't act on that emotionally charged Superficial Spark moment to talk immediately. If and when the individual does reply, it is very possible that you've moved on to messaging the next image. Plus, hearing someone's voice and being a part of the overall live interaction add to the meeting process. Reading a return text pales in comparison.

The limited preliminary action can throw off your whole dating progression. Remember, a person progresses out of the Bust-Down Worthy stage only after a certain level and type of information is shared. They move through the Friendship phase only after more information is exchanged and a specific type of rapport building takes place. Eventually, if all goes well, then you two can decide to exclusively date.

Well, what happens when you've barely interacted enough to sit firmly in Bust-Down territory (and by interact, we mean sending a few flirty messages back and forth), but you've got information, via their dating profile, conducive to being somewhere in the Friendship phase? *And*, you've never even spent real-world time in front of this person . . .

A rushed sense of progression can develop. You may think that you "know" someone well because of the profile information. Those are just words. They may be words that'll be congruent with the true person, but you won't know that early in the game, no matter how lengthy that profile is. Safe, smart dating involves taking your time to see if the person you're interested in can add up to all the rosy words they let fall from their lips. Dating apps, by their very design, promote skipping certain important developmental dating plateaus. They give uneducated daters a false sense of security, and for whatever reason, these daters seem more apt to trust much more quickly while going this online dating route.

If you're one of those folks who feel they require a dating app for some reason, you must be careful not to allow the dating app to retard many of the natural dating stages you *need* to go through in order to build a sufficiently secure and stable union. Your best bet is probably to engage these people you meet online in the real world and take them through the natural process of dating progression. Remember, you need to have a fortified understanding of yourself before all else. Don't get caught up in words, pretty pics, and profile information.

And be careful, online low-lives are a real thing.

CHAPTER 9

MY TYPE THIS, MY TYPE THAT

SELF, VULNERABILITY, COMMON INTERESTS, LONGEVITY

When people speak about their "type," what are they really referring to? Sure, someone could have an affinity to a certain car brand, or maybe even a type of bread they choose when shopping at the local corner store. But, what does it mean to have a type in the dating world? Also, how healthy, smart, and emotionally progressive is it to adhere to a supposed dating type? When do we need to abandon the ideology of a dating type?

So, what is your type? When we refer to a particular type in the dating world, we are basically talking about a particular person with a particular set of attributes. These qualities can be physical, mental, or even something shown on the emotional level that we are attracted to. These elements are clearly a matter of personal preference. There may be a few universal qualities that the majority of us are attracted to, which also lay the foundation for the basis of your attraction, but the other attributes definitely originate from personal affinities. Think of a row of townhomes. They all look similar, at the foundation. They all have the same number of floors. They all have the same number of bathrooms, windows, even light fixtures. The differences are based solely on the person or people living in the townhome.

Well, the development of a "dating type" is very similar. For the most part, we're all human, and we all have certain foundational wants and needs. No one openly wants an asshole. No one openly wants to date a guy who's going to treat them like shit. We do, however, all seem to like someone who's caring, someone who'll show that their mate means something more to them than a sizzling piece of butt meat. There are certain preferences that can be considered negative, but from the individual's point of view those preferences are very attractive. We will discuss this a little bit later. Yes, for the most part, the foundational elements are preferred across the board. The attributes sitting on top of that foundation are what separate the types of guys you'd go for from the types someone else would swoon over.

The Good, the Bad

If you recall, we discussed a while back the laundry list of attributes that someone needed to possess in order for you to be interested in dating them. This list, rooted in the superficial (which was explained in the chapter "Reasonable Expectations"), is the starting point for exploring what preferences constitute a type. After we've gotten past the superficial stage, and through the Bust-Down Worthy phase, certain attributes not linked to superficial thought begin to adopt a greater importance. These attributes sort of become a measuring stick as to how compatible you are with this potential mate sitting across from you. Closer examination of said attributes reveals something very interesting about you, about the way you work, and what makes you tick socially.

The word "type" connotes a pattern. When you think of a type in dating, you're referring to a set of attributes that someone is attracted to, or has been drawn to on multiple occasions. So by definition, and Sherlock Holmes–like deduction, your type is at its simplest the group of characteristics and attributes you go after the most. This is not to say that different combinations of certain attributes aren't attractive to you, but that you do tend to lean toward a certain collection of these qualities more often than not.

Some people may argue, "Hey, none of the girls I've dated looked remotely similar." Well, you're thinking only superficially, which is sooooooo first chapter. Try to keep up. Remember, once you've successfully reached the Friendship phase, you're effectively thinking with more than just your dick. As a matter of fact, you wouldn't have gotten out of the Bust-Down Worthy phase if your dick was the only thing stimulated.

If we were discussing the types you like to bed, then characteristics like "brunette," "huge dick," and "whirlwind tongue" would be important. Though we do have types that we show a pattern of aesthetic affinity for, here we are focusing more on other aspects. Elements of character that have to do with better defining someone as an individual are what we're looking at. So, it's okay if you're into brunettes with long hair and massive pectorals, but within that group there are specifics that you find more attractive. As you may be the person who likes brunettes with huge pectorals, you may also like those brunettes to be well read. Your buddy may like the same thing physically, but be more inclined to try dating the brunette who likes adventure. Sometimes your "type" isn't something that can be readily defined through aesthetic affinity only.

Take a look at your dating history. You'd probably lose a bet if you thought these previous flings didn't all have something in common. If you're reviewing the physical elements of each, and your past love interests don't connect, try looking at their other, more hidden qualities. You'll be surprised at the similarities. You'll also realize that a lot of the people you've dated have had something in common with someone else you previously messed around with. Therein hides your dating pattern.

Who's to say if your attraction to these similarities is rooted in something mystic, or even scientific? The important thing is that it exists at all. This can give you some insight into the good choices you have made over the years when it comes to dating. It can also clue you in on things you may need to tweak before going forward with your dating life.

We don't really need to spend much time reviewing the preferences pertaining to good qualities, but just so all the T's are crossed and the I's are dotted . . . We all know a good-quality type when we see or hear about them. He's close to his mother. She helps old people cross the street. Someone who's caring, thoughtful, intelligent, tolerant, understanding, dependable, honest, attentive, and a plethora of other greeting-card-ready words. Everyone knows what these are. Being adventurous, cultured, driven—we all understand these qualities. For the most part, most of us would like someone who has these as well as a bunch of other shining attributes. Looking for these qualities in a mate definitely means you're on the right track. These ain't the qualities you should be worried about.

The shitty side of someone, that's what you should be worried about. If you're not drawn to these types of elements in a person, consider yourself one levelheaded, lucky person. Most people, on some level, are attracted to the less-than-savory ingredients of the human psyche, along with the roses-and-champagne side. Those things about someone that would be considered detestable from the outside looking in can magically seem alluring when you're directly involved with that person.

Don't believe it?

How many times have you been inexplicably drawn to someone you know you shouldn't like? You know he's player but you give it a shot anyway. You know she's a bad girl, but you try to keep up with her lifestyle regardless of the signs. Let's be even more specific. In your younger dating life, maybe you liked thugs. Not some wannabe, jean-sagging loudmouth. No, you liked the dude who held up the corner. He had nothing going for him, but he had that outlaw appeal. So what is it? What's the allure? Why do we put on our best Icarus impressions and go zero to sixty straight for the flame? Well . . . this could be quite the lengthy conversation, but for the sake of getting to the point, let's, well, get to the point . . .

Most of us adhere to routine. Most of us, on some level, care about societal norms. Most of us would even consider ourselves straight-ish arrows. But, there is something to be said about the guy or girl who just doesn't give a rat's backside about conventional ways of thinking. They walk their own path, and they really don't care if you take the same journey or not. It's sexy as hell and quite magnetic to be around people like this. Because people like this can be rare, and because they don't really care to fit into societal norms, they can almost seem unattainable. And don't let them actually have nice personalities . . . Your emotions will be in a whole world of trouble. And though these folks shouldn't be considered "bad" or "trouble," the fact that their personalities make them emotionally distant can cause you issues down the road.

While viewing the world in a rebellious sort of way isn't necessarily a bad thing, many of us mistakenly view people doing legitimately bad things as going against the grain. The thug isn't naturally rebelling against social norms, he's just a fucktard who hasn't found a better way to live. The player isn't just a rake who's internally compelled to chase after people he's attracted to. He's a self-aware prick who knows exactly what he's doing when he attempts to seduce someone.

We don't even have to go to the previous extremes. Someone who's extremely selfish isn't the type of person you'd want to go after, but many of us do. Someone whose life is too busy because it's wrapped around work and personal advancement isn't the best candidate to interview for the position of new boo, but we still do. There are a number of glaring negativities that we somehow transform into positives . . . and we chase after them. Some of us are even conscious that we're behaving in a less-than-beneficial fashion.

But, we're attracted to these unavailable people all the same. You could very well *be* one of these people yourself. Somehow, our brains are, in a dysfunctional way, relating and grouping the no-good folks with those who actually march to their own percussion section.

The reason for this is equally as simple: we want what we can't have.

Why Can't I Have It?

This is Psychology 101. You want what you can't have. Because you can't have it, you want it even more. As a matter of fact, the thing that you can't have becomes even more attractive because you can't have it. Everyone likes money, but the poor man covets greenbacks far more desperately than the man who pays all his bills on time. It is what it is.

So, let's revisit exactly what your "type" is when it comes to dating.

If you're successful in dating, your type is whomever you want them to be.

If not, your type takes on a whole new dimension. To the less-than-successful dater, one can argue that your "type" is the person or people who possess a combination of characteristics you're attracted to, but aren't necessarily compatible with. The fact that you like those particular characteristics, wrapped up in a particular physical package, which you haven't been able to lock down, makes you want that package even more. Remember, we've already defined having a type as following a pattern in dating. The fact that a pattern exists shows that you aren't successful with people who have that certain combination of characteristics, right? If you were, you wouldn't be single, still going after what you perceive to be as your type. Also, you need to consider those bad preferences that were mentioned earlier. You're attracted to things you can't have and maybe even things you should not want to be anywhere near.

Let that sink in for a minute.

Consider the possibility that you're into your "type" only because you can't readily have it, which amplifies the want for it. If you repeatedly bomb when dealing with your type, consider making some changes in your dating life. What you're dealing with is a crazy, emotion-driven cycle that probably needs to be broken in order for you to meet someone who could truly fit with you.

Chasing your "type" can be a thankless cycle:

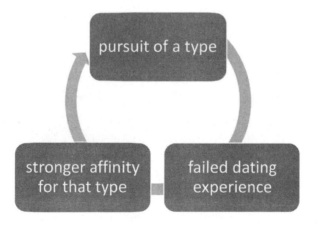

Some have dubbed it the "Cat with a String" theory. The idea of wanting someone or something you can't have is something we all can relate to. It makes more sense to call this a developmentally controlled substance effect . . . or something like that. The point is, once you get a taste of something you really like, you become obsessed with having it again. The harder it is to attain, the more you want it. It could almost be considered a mild addiction of sorts.

The pivotal point in this cycle is actually when you fail at the dating experience. Relationships don't crumble right away, so you actually get a moment or two to enjoy that person, that "type" you think you like. Suddenly, when things end, you begin to reminisce over the good aspects about your relationship. You begin to dwell on the characteristics of your former mate. Subconsciously or not, you begin to look for a new person possessing those qualities you lost when your former mate walked away. The pursuit of something you once had greatly strengthens your attraction to that something.

Wash, Rinse, Repeat

We're supposed to grow and gain worldly experience. With that experience, we're supposed to make better choices. One would hope that these experiences we gain over time would also give us a better internal understanding. With that internal comprehension, we should have a better understanding of how we fit socially in the world. This includes the decisions we make when it comes to dating.

We are ever-evolving creatures. As we get older and gain more experience, our viewpoints in life can begin to change. You may not want to be a fireman when you actually grow up. The things we used to find important as children are not necessarily going to carry as much weight for us as adults. The crucial elements needed in a potential mate when you were fourteen years old will not be the same make-or-break qualities you'll need in that person as an adult.

Ideally, by the time you reach adulthood, you should know enough about yourself to actually wade through the shit and find a good mate. But, because we aren't taught to explore ourselves, many of us are at a disadvantage socially, specifically in the dating world. We latch on to the people we believe to be our type and often look past those who would better fit us.

As stated in earlier chapters, the more you know about yourself, the more proactive and conscious a decision you can make in finding someone who is actually compatible. The logical side of your brain works in conjunction with the emotional side. Your heart and head balance each other out so that your "type" is actually, well, your type . . . not a string of unattainable folks with things that you happen to like about them. But, as it stands, when you don't know about yourself well enough, the emotional side of your brain rules and you end up getting caught in the aforementioned cycle of chasing down your supposed type.

Many of us, without the help of internal exploration, continue to go through life collecting experiences, but not being able to apply those experiences to ourselves. We sort of turn a blind eye to the very mistakes we tend to make, hence engaging in the same dating cycles over and over. When you were in high school, unless you were one of the cool kids, you probably developed a "type." You spent time chasing after said type throughout your high school career.

When you reached college age, your experiences dictated that certain aspects of someone's character would have a higher level of importance than others. Hopefully, those characteristics were more substantial than superficial, because you'd had enough experience to realize a good mate is made up of deeper stuff than just good hair and huge muscles by this point. If you'd spent a decent amount of time exploring yourself, you'd have had a good chance of meeting a decent mate. If not, you'd have ended up in another "type" cycle. The same is probably going on right this very minute if you have not spent a considerable amount of time finding out who you are.

The future looks to be just about the same . . .

If you still find yourself playing dating musical chairs with the clones of previous relationships, you have to learn how to break the cycle. The first step in breaking this detrimental dating rotation is to admit that you actually go after people who may not be compatible with you. It's okay to be attracted to certain characteristics, but if these qualities don't mesh with the person you are, then it is also okay to try something different. You never know, you may begin to respect other attributes that you never even considered before. Maybe the so-called boring guy offers you the stability you so desperately crave but can't receive from the Billy Bad-Ass you think is your type. You can either spend the rest of your life playing relationship tag, or be proactive and fix the holes in your dating and relationship armor.

Game Reset

If you take anything away from this manual at all, take this: Everything starts with you. No matter what you're talking about, or what aspect of life you're looking at, everything starts with you. You can't have a relationship without you in it. Your perspective is always from the inside looking outward. We can't help but to internalize everything. The good, the bad, we take everything in. We process this information, and then figure out how to proceed based on our analyses. When it comes to love and matters of the heart, however, we tend to lean toward the idealistic and shun the realistic. Foggy brains and full nuts lead to some bad decisions at times.

In order to discontinue your best Formula One racer impersonation—you know, going around in circles chasing your type?—more self-examination is needed. Yes, even more self-evaluation. Remember, dating and relationships ultimately begin with you, with who you are as a person. Go back to that list of attributes. By now, you should've separated those qualities into the three categories. Take a look at those quality combinations you find yourself going after most often. Out of those particular groupings, pick the qualities that you like, but don't necessarily like you back. File that information away in the back of your mind, to be used soon.

Now, when you meet someone new, take note when they display those flashy characteristics that look good in your mind, but morph into disgusting creatures when viewed in the real world. This timeline is totally up to you, but you need to engage it at some point. When a certain negative quality is displayed too often, by the same person or multiple interests, make note of it. Strike this quality from your list of desired attributes. After a period of time, set by you, go back and look to see how many of those characteristics from your supposed type still exist. If your list looks like a bachelor's fridge after striking down so many attributes, it's time to rebuild your type.

Think dating trial and error. Well, most dating is trial and error anyway, but because you've spent the time exploring who you are and hopefully eliminating many of the negative aspects of people's characters within your dating search, you'll be better prepared. At this point you may be playing the numbers game, but those numbers will be significantly lower because you've made a conscious effort to modify the way you date by actively looking for attributes that mesh better with the person you are.

You can't just go through the motions, however. You need to truly believe that you deserve a mate who'll complement and respect your differences, while using your similarities to build a strong bond together. You need to realize that your previous type is nothing more than a roller coaster that you keep paying emotionally to ride. Breaking the negative cycle of dating starts with you believing that you don't belong in the cycle, period.

By exposing yourself to things that stimulate your passions, you foster a better understanding of yourself (check out the chapter "Self and Independence"). By surrounding yourself with people who share these passions, you have a better chance of meeting someone you'll really click with. You'll begin to see that the "type" you've been chasing down for your entire dating life is nothing more than a pretty distraction rooted in that silly laundry list of characteristics that have no bearing on who you really are as a person. Your previous type is nothing more than another learning experience to be applied to your dating life, assisting you in becoming a more educated dater.

Wants Equals Needs

Here's the relatively tricky part. How do you convince yourself that you want what you need? Sounds confusing, but it's not. Basically, how can you shift your brain, and get your heart in line with the idea that your needs outweigh your wants? Therefore, you should want your needs more than your wants, get it? We all know how cloudy our brains can get when we're smitten with someone, so getting past this obstacle may not be a walk in the park. A lot of this internal transition comes from the experience of time. The more you learn, the more you go through, the more you realize that some of the dumb shit you thought you wanted is rather meaningless in the current stage of your life. Hopefully, if this is your issue, you can also shake the want for those negative attributes in a mate we discussed earlier. It's easy enough to say certain things are bad. It's harder still to let go of certain things, especially when they can be so tempting.

Of course, most of these things are left up to your change in preference, so what you may not need still may hold weight with someone else's dating choices.

Also, it should be noted that some superficiality is necessary when choosing a mate. Refer to the first chapter for a better understanding of this fact. If someone suggests you go after a potential mate whom you have no physical attraction to whatsoever, never listen to them again. Some sort of physical attraction is definitely necessary. The guy doesn't have to be GQ Model #1, but you should have some sort of aesthetic affinity for the man. That "Beauty and the Beast" crap is a fairy tale. Granted, you can become more attracted to someone over time because of who they really are, but if there's no electricity at all . . . that's a hard mountain to climb.

Now that all that's out of the way, let's get to the real issue, your self-worth. The only way to truly convince yourself that needs should be wants is by believing that you're worth more. When it comes to dating and relationships, many people let things slide, important things, just to catch and keep a mate. No one is suggesting that compromise isn't needed to keep a relationship healthy, but certain things aren't up for consideration.

Anything involving basic human respect should never be brushed to the side. How many one-sided relationships have you been a part of, or how many have you seen where someone's feelings, needs, and even wants were cast down in order to keep the other person happy? It happens all of the time. One person values their mate more than they value themselves, while the mate values their own happiness. Hopefully, the best-case scenario is that the slighted individual in the relationship catches on and actively makes changes. This could be by communicating this feeling of secondary citizenship to the love interest, or by walking away if the scenario is too far gone. Either way, realization of self-worth causes the change.

So, to take it a step further, a strong sense of self-worth will demand that you get what you need in a relationship. You simply won't settle for less, because you won't want less. Believing in the importance of you is truly the only way to break that silly dating cycle and to convince yourself that your needs should be more important than your wants.

Development of this high self-esteem, because of your self-exploration, will cause you to go after people who have what you need in a relationship because you'll realize you're worth finding that person who truly complements you. Ultimately, this change in mind-set will lead to . . .

Elimination of the Superficial Mind-Set

Well, to a certain extent. Sure, as stated before, you need an initial attraction rooted in the superficial. But, the superficial mind-set that may have previously ruled your dating thought process will begin to die off. Big muscles won't be nearly as attractive as a big heart. Perfect skin and model hair will take a backseat to the mate who shares your passions and enjoys your differences. You'll notice that your focus won't be fixated on keeping someone around; it'll be dialed in to finding new adventures with this person who wouldn't want to be anywhere else. All of this will be because you made the conscious decision to invest in yourself. You get what you give, so the better and more well-rounded you are, the higher caliber of person you stand the chance to meet and keep. Arguably, even more important is the fact that you'll be much more fortified in deflecting the people you don't need to be dealing with.

Not Missing Your Soul Mate

We can sit around all day and discuss the idea of "the One." You know, the one person created just for you. The soul mate. Some people believe in this, others don't. Though the idea that one person in six billion is made especially for you is far-fetched, and frankly a little sad, this notion does promote the idea of not settling for less than the right person.

After going through your self-evaluation, it is more probable—and much more optimistic—to believe that out of six billion folks on the planet, there are multiple people with the right combination of physical and internal attributes who'll match with you.

And that is what a soul mate really is. The soul mate isn't something mystical. The soul mate is quite tangible. The feelings manifested through your union with a soul mate can border on the mystical, but defining a soul mate is quite simple. Constructing relationships is like building houses. The foundation is a strong mutual caring between the two of you. Your similarities act as the framework. Respecting and exploring your differences while finding new mutual interests and adventures is the drywall that strengthens and fills in the gaps, and actually allows you to expand your love for one another. But that's not all. Something is still missing. The mortar. Your soul mate is the one who has the right emotional glue to hold everything together.

The mortar, so to speak, is the undying willingness to make things work. A true soul mate is the person who has the qualities you need and the resolve to work with you to fortify your relationship. The soul mate knows your union can never be perfect, because neither one of you is perfect, but the soul mate is willing to build, repair, and support. Above all else, the soul mate will try their hardest to see the world through your eyes. They'll put your needs, wants, and passions above their own because their very well-being is tied into you striving. If you have someone like this, then they can very well be the soul mate you need. Everything else is up to you—up to you to be for them what they want to be for you. There's nothing magical about it, just the will and drive to make things work.

So don't miss out on a soul mate . . .

People do this all the time. Taking the opportunity to read this manual shows that you really want to meet someone worthwhile. Most people probably want to do the same. The problem is, they get in their own way. This is why so much time is spent teaching you to eliminate the distractions and would-be negative elements in your life. This is also why self-exploration is promoted so heavily. By better knowing yourself, and by brushing off any unneeded distraction, you can create a clearer path to your goal of finding the right person.

Shedding the silly laundry list, easing up on unfair expectations, and modifying your thought process in regard to what you need in a relationship are major pillars in constructing the right you for the right person. Don't bother spending time with people you *know* it won't work out with either; all they'll do is take up time and for no reason. They're like alcohol. They may look and even taste good, but they add no nutritional value to a healthy love life.

Fuck buddies as well. They're fun, and sometimes we just need that release, but if you think you've found a good mate, drop the f-buddy like the f-bomb. Even if you want to lie to yourself about the absence of feelings with your fuck-buddy, it's not true. There's always a level of attachment involved, at least from one side or the other. Emotions are like a rubber band. They can stretch only so far before something pops back and stings your ass. Focus your emotional energies on the love interest you think will become someone special. If it doesn't work out, then the fuck-buddy can resume the position. Don't deal with them when you're trying to construct a committed relationship, because they'll just cause unneeded distraction later.

The less distraction you have, and the more positive reinforcement, the better chance you have of getting whom and what you want.

CHAPTER 10

RISK AND VULNERABILITY

TRUST, RISK, VULNERABILITY, EMPATHY

Risk, by definition, is the likelihood of some sort of detriment, forfeiture, suffering, or danger to befall you. The likelihood that something of a negative nature may happen to you leaves you in a vulnerable state. The greater the risk, the greater the chance that you will be met by this suffering or loss. Also, the greater the risk, the greater the loss if something goes wrong. Spending two bucks on your city's lottery every week would be considered very low risk, because you're betting only $2. Riding to Vegas and dropping your college tuition on the blackjack table is a little riskier. The idea of risk is so prevalent in society that even Fortune 500 companies have departments dedicated to the calculation and analysis of risk. There are people in those departments who are paid a decent piece of change to show companies how to minimize risk, that is, minimize the chance for detriment, forfeiture, suffering, or danger to befall the company.

On the other side of the same coin is vulnerability. If risk is the likelihood of something going south on you, then vulnerability is how susceptible you are to being in some way damaged by something negative happening to you. Vulnerability is the thin spot in the armor, so to speak. The greater the risk, the greater the possible vulnerability.

Why are we so worried about vulnerability and risk? Because we're trying to protect something. Obviously, what you'd be trying to protect on an individual level and what a huge corporate conglomerate would be shielding are quite different. But, both parties are trying to protect something. In suit-and-tie speak, that something in need of protection would be known as an asset. So, the beefing up on the understanding of risk and the minimizing of vulnerability are all to protect something you hold dear.

And then there is the threat. In business terms, the threat is what the company is preparing for. The reason companies have risk management teams, the reason you look both ways before crossing the street, is the threat. The threat is that outside entity, whatever it may be, that can cause damage. It is the thing that can manipulate the thin spots in your armor. If left unchallenged, via risk management and such, the threat is that driving force that can get to your asset . . . the thing you're trying to protect the most.

The obsession with preventing risk and neutralizing threats is a no-brainer. No one wants something they put a lot of work into, including bodily fluids . . . no, not those bodily fluids . . . to be torn down because of a lack of planning or protection. No matter where you look in society, steps have been taken to prevent risk. Cops carry guns. Farmers use pesticides. Cars have air bags and bumpers. People use condoms. All of these things are for protection against the chance of suffering or loss, and in some cases long, excruciatingly painful loss (like having kids).

The bottom line is that no one wants to be vulnerable.

Risk and Relationships

If risk is defined as the probability of something negative happening to you by the exploitation of your vulnerabilities, how do we fine-tune the explanation for the risks in relationships? We define risk in three parts when we look at it in terms of relationships. Well, there is the risk of a threat from an external source. There is the risk tied to overexposing your asset to the outside world, or an uncontrollable or unforeseeable threat. Then there is the risk of not being able to control your asset, and therefore not being able to properly protect that asset.

But why, why wouldn't you be able to control your own asset? We will discuss this shortly.

A risk in the dating game isn't as cut-and-dry as the risks met in other areas of life. In other areas, people spend time and resources protecting the asset. Risk management exists solely for the purpose of strengthening vulnerabilities and neutralizing threats, most times before the threat even reveals itself. There is, however, a huge fundamental difference with relationship risk in comparison to other types of risk, because the asset you're charged to protect is indeed your very own heart.

In other types of risk, the asset is a stand-alone entity. It could be money, or technology, or something else that wouldn't be readily able to recognize the threats coming after it. With relationship risk you have to stand strong on three different fronts. Again, you have to protect your asset from the outside threats coming after it. You have to know when to expose the asset to the outside world. And finally, you have to keep the asset from running wild. Yes, relationship risk management is hugely based on controlling your asset and keeping it from charging full speed toward the very threats you're trying to protect it from.

Think of this manual, in large part, as a relationship risk manual.

With that being said, let's examine the three borders you'll be guarding to protect that asset of yours. The first and most obvious threat is an external threat. In the dating and relationship game, not all advances are considered threats. You have the nice folks with good intentions, many of whom end up becoming platonic buddies because they're just too nice. Everyone's had these scenarios, and everyone's probably been on both sides of this equation. No, the external threat being referred to is the person you're attracted to who shows clear signs that they may not be good for you. If you recall the laundry list of characteristics, then you should remember the whole section dedicated to pointing out the attractive yet negative qualities. These are the characters being referred to. Your "type." That elusive yet incredibly attractive person who continues to draw you in and eventually leaves you feeling empty . . . and looking for someone just like them. This type of risk is defined as knowing the worst about someone yet still respecting and wanting them regardless of the possibility of a negative outcome.

Within this risk set are two subsets:

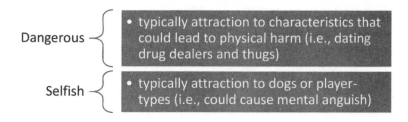

Dangerous — • typically attraction to characteristics that could lead to physical harm (i.e., dating drug dealers and thugs)

Selfish — • typically attraction to dogs or player-types (i.e., could cause mental anguish)

Clearly, both risks can cause you considerable pain. Also, it should be noted that a hybrid jerk-off possessing characteristics from both subsets has been known to exist as well. Actively avoid clowns like this at all costs. They're more trouble than they're worth.

The second type of risk is overexposure of the asset. In short, you do not want to become jaded. The world is a hard place, and it's full to the brim with self-centered assholes. The dating game is about tactfully navigating through the jerks and fucktards and finding someone you click with, unless of course you're one of the jerks or fucktards. In which case, you're doing your job quite well. Overexposure to too many negative aspects of the dating world can have you adopt an "all people ain't shit" attitude. This can, and oftentimes does, shut people down. They begin to feel like everyone's bad—or even worse, their self-esteem can take a major hit. A good person, with enough dating mishaps under the belt, may begin to believe that there is something seriously wrong internally. They may begin to feel that they have no place in the dating world. They may feel that they should just be alone to avoid the frustration and heartache that is sure to follow from trying to meet someone. There's nothing worse than one of those cyclical, self-fulfilling prophecies.

The third risk you'll need to guard against is the potential stubbornness of your heart. Simply put, your heart wants what it wants. If compelled it'll go running—not walking, but running—toward what it wants. Sometimes, no degree of common sense or previous experience can corral the locomotive that is your body's engine. Mastering your heart is an ongoing task. No one is perfect, and many of the so-called experts even slide back into a negative experience or two. But, learning to fortify your heart is the best way to protect this vital asset.

Your Asset

You're probably thinking, "I didn't pick up this manual to take a Risk Management 101 course." And though you're absolutely right, calm down a second and give the idea a chance to work itself out. It is human nature to want to protect yourself. Protection is the way we have survived and advanced as a species for the umpteen number of years we have existed. Arguably, figuring out how to protect ourselves, how to assess a situation and create the best outcome for that situation, is the human being's greatest adaptation. Everything we do, at a base level, is for the fortification of self. We internally apply our own risk management in all areas of life to limit our vulnerability in those areas. We do things for job security. We walk with mace in our purses to our cars in dark parking lots. We try to secure as much money as possible in order to weather any financial storm that may try to overtake us. We are constantly building, and fortifying, and rebuilding our mental and physical armor.

It should come as a surprise then that across the board men and women alike can have the hardest time when it comes to asset fortification and protection in relationships. Once again, it's the heart. When the heart is left to its own devices unchecked, then we find ourselves with more than our asses exposed.

The heart. It is the main thing we want to protect in a relationship, yet it is the part of you that needs to be allowed freedom in order to help develop the intimate bonds crucial to the establishment of a working union. As you know, the brain alone can't generate a lasting love affair. You need the healthy balance of both heart and head to build something substantial.

As you know from at least one previous experience, however, the heart is never an easy thing to control, especially when you meet that person who has the right combination of qualities you're drawn to. As we discussed in an earlier chapter, those qualities, in that combination, may not be the best for you, but . . . imagine trudging through a desert with no food or water, then suddenly stumbling across your favorite fast-food joint. An oasis of fried foods and carbonated beverages is now at your disposal. You know it ain't good for you, but it tastes damn good, and it'll sustain you for a time. You'll feel as if you've found what you needed even if deep down in your brain, common sense is telling you no. That is your heart, ladies and gentleman . . . filled with emotional impulse, rooted in the superficial, and often stimulated by aesthetically pleasing things. Your heart sounds a lot like an inquisitive toddler, doesn't it? It cannot be allowed to wander the wilderness that is dating all alone.

Because your heart thrives on the raw and the visceral, how can you ever hope to get through to it? The heart doesn't deal in common sense. Similar to that rambunctious toddler, it wants what it wants. This is why, when left unchecked, your heart can get you in a whole world of shit. So again, how does one utilize a leash equipped with a choker to train that wild beast you have bouncing around in your chest?

The brain . . .

Your Risk Manager

The yin to your heart's yang is your brain. Where your heart can't help but to act on pure impulse, your brain has the ability to better assess situations, helping you make better decisions. It is because of this fact that your brain alone should act as your risk manager. The problem is,

istock/Baluchis

many people need to be taught how to see a clear picture of the dating game in order for their brains to be any use in risk management and vulnerability fortification. You know what they say, "If you don't use it, you lose it." A better saying in this case would be, "If you don't train it, you won't gain it." Err, or something like that.

Seriously, though, your brain does need to be trained, specifically in self-understanding. The more you train it, the more you gain (self-understanding). The reason so much emphasis is placed on self-understanding in this very manual is because you need to realize and accept the utter importance of understanding yourself. Self-understanding, improving on self-understanding, is the starting point for everything you do. The better you understand yourself, the better decisions you'll make in regard to how you fit in the world. This unswervingly includes the decisions you'll make in matters of the heart.

Risk management, as it stands in the dating world, is all about self-understanding. Just look at the training you've received thus far. Globally, you've learned the way people interact with each other in an intimate capacity. You've learned how people progress through the dating phases. You've learned the tug-of-war between the heart and head in reference to dating and the different dating stages. You've also learned the typical ways in which the human brain attempts to categorize everyone and everything.

On a specific level, you've learned to ascertain exactly how *you* function socially overall, and in dating and relationships explicitly. You've dissected your specific laundry lists needed and wanted qualities in a potential mate. You've also learned how to better categorize those qualities to help you make stronger decisions in selecting a mate. You've learned the difference between reasonable and outlandishly stupid expectations.

You've even spent time learning about ways of exploring yourself as a whole. You now have an idea as to how to foster your passions, satisfy your needs, and obtain your wants. You've learned about your weaknesses of self and your weaknesses when it comes to attraction to those you'd call a potential mate.

But for what?

Everything that you've read thus far is your Relationship Risk Management 300 Level coursework. This is your risk analysis. This is understanding your vulnerabilities in order to fortify them. This is being able to identify those things that may stand as a threat to you in the dating world. You have accumulated all of this information for your mental fortification. The only way to develop a strong dating risk management program is to put these words into action in the real world. This is your guide to self-understanding and fortification. This is the outline to training your brain and developing a strong risk management system to better protect your heart.

Imagine those security programs you install on your laptop. You know they sort of create a check system for everything you do with your computer. Are you sure you want to go to this website? Are you certain the software you want to install is safe? Those security programs scrutinize every little thing you do. You paid about sixty bucks for this software to cover your ass, and that's exactly what it's going to do. Hell, some security programs won't even allow you to go to websites you viewed before the security installation. It's like the security program is openly telling you what a dumb idea it is to revisit silly shit from the past.

Well, all of that, up there, is what your brain will do after proper training and conditioning . . .

Protection on Three Fronts

Every time your heart is threatened on one of the three fronts, your brain will kick in and help you think a little more clearly about matters of the heart. "Uh oh, he's a player. Watch out. Red flag. Here are the signs." Or, "Wait a minute, you're being a little too jaded. She's a nice girl. Try to give her a chance." Or, "Oh, hell no, I know you ain't thinkin' of fuckin' with Steve's stupid ass again. Don't be a fuck-boy toy."

For the external threats as well as threats from your heart, your brain will act as an archive to remind you of similar threats you had in the past. Red flags are those indicators. You wouldn't even know what a Red flag is if you hadn't experienced a similarly shitty scenario at some time before. Your brain will quickly remind you of that shitty time.

As far as any threat originating from overexposure and jading, your brain takes a rather opposite approach. When the heart is filled with hate and mistrust and hurt, and damage in general, the owner of said heart truly does develop a different viewpoint on life. The heart shuts down. Left unchecked, that bleak outlook can bleed into the brain and poison it. Have you ever seen those people who seem to carry a perpetual dark cloud over their heads? Have you ever wondered why that cloud seems fixed?

Nine times out of ten, the person using that dark cloud as fashionable headwear has had something, or multiple things, happen to them that affected them so negatively that their heart chose to build a wall. The origin of their pain doesn't have to be relationship based, but many times, that's exactly what it is. Because thinking only with the heart means thinking only with emotion, rational thought can go out of the window. All the heart knows is that it's been hurt. It doesn't want that again, so without cranial supervision, the heart can go apeshit. "I'll just convince my owner that it's a far better idea to not trust anyone. We'll never be hurt again, because we won't allow anyone in."

Of course, you know as well as the next man that this sort of emotional isolation can be like a cancer . . . eating away at a person from the inside out. On the outside they may seem rock solid, but internally, they're in a very sad state. They're isolated. They're in a prison. This is why training your brain to counteract this poisonous activity is so important. Self-exploration here is not so much for finding out things about yourself that make you awesome. The crucial element here is self-exploration as a source of fortification for you as a whole. You need to train your brain to tell your heart that just because you've been hurt before doesn't guarantee you'll be hurt again. If you're hurt again, it doesn't diminish the extreme value of your self-worth. Your brain sort of allows your heart to harden selectively because of past pain, but not totally because of fear of future anguish.

The properly trained brain will act as that mental prophylactic charged with protecting you from all the fucking the world will try to do to you.

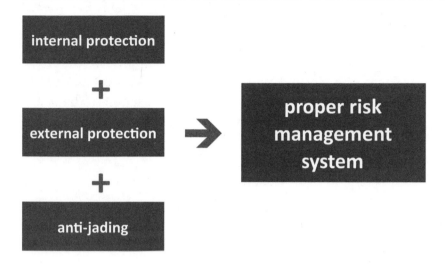

As you can see from the model, proper risk management is three equal parts external protection, internal fortification, and knowing exactly when to expose your heart to the outside world. It is a balancing act that only the person truly in tune with himself or herself will be able to pull off effectively.

The more you know about yourself, the more negative influences you'll be able to block, suppress, or just plain eradicate from your life, creating a much more benign environment for your heart to thrive in. Remember, happiness and being content with your place in life start with you. The more you know about yourself, the better you operate in the world. The more you know about yourself, the easier it is to protect yourself from internal and external threats. See the connection? By engaging in the activities previously described throughout the chapters of this manual, you're slowly making yourself a rather impervious force in the social world.

Knowing Your Vulnerabilities and Covering Your Ass

Here is yet another reason why self-exploration is important. Knowing yourself isn't just about fostering your passions and promoting your good qualities. It's also about identifying those truly negative characteristics you've developed and working on improving them. Self-understanding is also about identifying weaknesses you have and creating an internal support system to help combat those weaknesses.

Of course, these types of discoveries are person specific. This is why you've spent so much time exploring who you are in previous chapters. The nature and severity of your particular vulnerabilities are also pretty person specific. The alleviation of these relationship ailments will vary from person to person as well.

Though the process of targeting and eliminating a vulnerability isn't always a linear equation, this handy little schematic describes how we can go about targeting and alleviating a personal relationship problem or negative characteristic.

Clearly, the first step would be to find that less-than-appealing characteristic or relationship issue you seem to continue to struggle with. Ways to identify these things are outlined in the previous chapters. So, you've targeted an issue. Let's just say you have an issue with giving up the booty a little too quickly during your progression through the dating phase. You've looked back on your dating history and realize that you seem to fall quickly for words and don't wait around long enough to see whether or not congruent actions will follow. With your newly conditioned risk management brain, you decide to make a conscious effort not to peel off your underwear until you've removed enough of your potential mate's outer layers.

The follow-up step would be to fight your urge to give it up too quickly. This doesn't mean playing hard to get, and it doesn't mean acting like you're not interested. What it does mean is, when the urge to play naked Twister pops up in your heart, you'll activate your security program. You'll ask yourself to review the dating progression model.

You'll analyze whether or not you guys have built a rapport conducive to being more than just fuck buddies. What do you know about them, and what do they know about you? Does this person do the things you need them to do for you to feel comfortable bedding them? Does this person fit into the newfound information you know about yourself? Once you can honestly satisfy the analyses, you're in a better place to get naked.

Maintenance for this type of issue isn't difficult. It's just a matter of observation. Does your potential mate do things to get something back from you? In other words, was he or she nice to you in the beginning only to get in your pants? A little bit later on, did this person show kindness and altruism only to get something out of you? Are pacification tactics used to keep you pseudo-happy? Don't make the mistake of thinking this tactic is for monitoring your potential mate. Oh no. This is to monitor you. This tactic is to make sure you're getting just as hung up on genuine action as you are with beautiful verbiage.

Say the targeted issue you want to work on is an overwhelming shyness. You've noticed, through a thorough review of past situations, that shyness has kept you from advancement in all social avenues, including the dating game. How do you get over this? This isn't always an easy fix. Some people need psychiatric assistance with debilitating shyness. Those with a crippling level of shyness may need other medical help of some sort. Even still, after they've gotten over that major mental hump, these people may utilize a similar plan of attack to suppress the shyness.

Shyness is one of those things that never fully leaves you. It is a legitimate characteristic and a part of who you are. You should learn to embrace it at some point in your life, but if it's interfering with your personal advancement, you do need to learn when and where to suppress it. As stated earlier, everyone is different. Some may just run head-first into a room of people and begin talking to everyone. We'll make the assumption that you're of moderate temperament. With that being said, your best bet may be to take a public speaking class. But, along with taking that class, you should apply what you learned in it to real-world settings. And, because we're talking about dating and relationships here, the real-world settings should be the ones that promote social interaction. D8able functions are always geared toward putting people in front of others so they can mingle.

How do you maintain your newfound suppressed shyness? Simply go to as many social functions as possible. The more you fight the want to tuck your head back into your shell, the easier it'll get to control the shyness. Your reluctance to be social may pop up every now and again, but you'll definitely notice a difference in your overall comfort level in dealing with people generally, as well as in your dating endeavors.

Okay, okay last example. Through a deep and profound research session, you've found that you have an issue with meeting people who actually have anything in common with you. Lucky for you, this is probably the easiest issue to remedy. The Internet is your friend.

Simply jump online or look in the ad section of your local newspaper (do people still read newspapers, like, actual paper newspapers?!). Do a search for groups that are involved in things you like to do. For instance, you like hiking? Look up hiking organizations. There are groups for literally anything you'd want to do. If you can't find a group, make your own and publicize it on social media. You're bound to meet people doing this.

The maintenance for this particular issue would be partaking in the activities you enjoy engaging in anyway. Find more groups. Explore different passions. Not only will you be doing things you enjoy, you'll also ultimately be meeting people and forging relationships of a platonic and intimate nature as well. More friends and more potential mates. Seems like a winning situation all the way around.

As stated earlier, your approach to removing certain recurring relationship issues from your life may not have such a linear progression, but at some point, you will hit each of these pit stops. The more info you have floating around in your brain about yourself, the better chance you have of plugging those holes in your armor.

Dysfunctional Risk Management

In an attempt to protect yourself, you should make sure not to engage in dysfunctional ways of relationship risk management. We discussed an example of this a little bit earlier. As with most decisions regarding the heart, there are multiple routes to the same end goal. The problem with a dysfunctional way of thinking is that you run the risk of ending up in an emotional dead end. You begin to think only with the heart, which is fueled by raw emotion. Emotion-filled decisions, especially the decisions backed by negative emotion, very rarely end well.

When you don't have your brain working in unison with your heart, the ability to clearly evaluate your scenario becomes stunted. Again, one of the major reasons so much time is spent on self-understanding is so you can better handle extreme times of emotional stress caused by dating. Your self-worth is everything during these periods because outside influences as well as a wavering self-esteem can cause you to doubt yourself during these times of relationship trauma. While your heart is freaking out, swimming through the sea of emotions, your developed risk-management-trained brain is supposed to keep you levelheaded.

Dysfunctional relationship risk management originates from the overpowering effect a developed heart has over the underdeveloped brain. Instead of the brain balancing things out, reassuring the heart of your self-worth, your heart is allowed to run amok. If you haven't spent enough time developing your self-esteem through self-exploration, you don't have that deep-rooted understanding of yourself. You can't think clearly about something you don't know much about. You can't balance out your heart's want to have a temper tantrum.

That doesn't mean people with developed self-understanding don't have moments of emotional hurricanes, but the likelihood of bouncing back from shitty relationship pitfalls is a lot greater with greater self-understanding.

Powerful Vulnerability

When we hear the term "vulnerability," many of us make the mistake of associating it with negative connotations. "Vulnerability" is often used synonymously with terms like "weakness" or "frailty." These words have no place together. A vulnerability is basically an aspect of your life you aren't quite that strong in. In relationship terms, a vulnerability may be a recurring mistake you make with the types of people you go for. It could be a recurring mode of operation that isn't yielding the results you want. Vulnerability is not weakness; it is a work in progress. It becomes a weakness only if you treat it like one . . . And since no one is technically perfect, we should all be using our vulnerabilities as stages for learning and improvement.

Let's put it this way: If we had no vulnerabilities, there would be no need for risk management. There would be no need for self-exploration. There would be no such thing as being a unique individual. Our vulnerabilities define us as much as our strengths and passions do. They're good starting points for personal growth.

Acknowledging a vulnerability is not weakness either. When you find a flaw and decide to work on it, you're proactively working on getting better at something. Self-improvement is something we all need to do, but so many of us can't admit it. Finding and attempting to rectify your flaws puts you ahead of the pack, especially when it comes to improving your game on the dating field.

CHAPTER 11

SEX AND SELF

SELF, TRUST, RESPECT, VULNERABILITY, RISKS, SEX, EMPATHY

Welcome to the high-stakes round. Sex . . . and self, but let's get into the sex. When we think of dating and relationships, no one wants to readily admit this, but sex is *the* centerpiece. Sure, you want to find that person who can captivate your mind, but you also want that person to simultaneously engulf your body in a favorable emotional combustion . . . leading to the physical manifestation of some bed-melting fucksational sexytime.

Yes, sex is the centerpiece, and rightfully so. If you look at the path of most relationships, and you look at the focus of most dating and relationship advice, what do people put most stock in? It's the sex. From all angles, it's the sex. You've got advice ranging from how to get it quickly to how to guard your sex from falling into the wrong hands.

People may not want to admit it, but sex, the act of having it, the burning desire to get it, and sexual compatibility are very weighty in a relationship. Why do you think someone can stay in a shitty relationship for so long when the sex is good? Ummm, because the sex is good. People conceivably connect on three planes. Ideally, for an intimate relationship to work, you'd want a mental connection. You'd also want a spiritual connection. Last, and certainly not least, is that physical connection . . . Sex is the manifestation of the physical connection.

Each one of these connections builds a bond between you and your mate. Once these bonds are made, they support and feed off each other (we will discuss this shortly). Other than this, these bonds are not similar to each other in any way. Because of this, when one of these bonds is lacking in a relationship, you crave that specific bond.

Here's the thing: physical attraction happens first, above all else. Remember the dating progression model discussed earlier? Physical attraction, on some level, appears long before any of the other bonds are being created. This means the idea of a physical connection, even if it's just a whisper in the early goings, is still in you . . . poking you, prodding you, wanting you to get closer to this new person in front of you.

Granted, sex means more when you have the mental and spiritual components of you and your love interest aligned as well, but you know just as well as the next person that physical attraction is what starts the whole process. The superficial side of you gets to work, and hopefully the rest of you follows. Physical attraction is the catalyst for everything else that will follow. It can also be considered one of the pillars of the foundation that everything else is built upon. As you progress through your dating journey, the want for physical intimacy isn't going to die out. If anything, this want will grow, especially if you perceive things to be going well with your potential mate.

The trick is being able to tell whether or not things are going well— that is, if both you and your potential significant other are on the same page.

On Guard

Sex, though a major part of physical attraction, is that element of relationship development that most dating consultants would tell you to ignore, at least earlier on. We all know full well that sex will always be that huge elephant in the back of the room. Sex isn't silent either. It may be in the back of the room, but it keeps eyeing you, and it wants you to know that it's eyeing you. It wants you to know that eventually, eventually you will give in. Even still, you are taught that engaging in sex too quickly isn't the best way to go.

You are taught to fortify the other fledgling bonds between you and your mate. Why is this? Think of it as a best-practice mode of operation for protecting you from getting hurt. The idea is pretty simple. In the dating world, the more you know about the person you're dating, the better. Mutual exploration leads either to bond building or to repelling each other.

Even with our dating progression model, we show that in order to build a strong relationship, the bonds are being built simultaneously on different planes. Although we initially begin with the Superficial Spark and physical attraction, in order to progress out of the Bust-Down Worthy phase and into the Friendship phase, the mental bond needs to be built as well. As the mental bond is being constructed through rapport building, as described in earlier chapters, you are continuing the construction of the physical bond simultaneously. As these two bonds continue to progress, the spiritual, or higher-level, bond begins to develop as well, while you continue to build and fortify the other two bonds. Get it?

In other words, once you've collected enough info and done enough rapport building for each bond, another bond begins to grow in succession. Eventually, you're building bonds on the three planes simultaneously, like so:

Physical Bond Progression

The Superficial Spark initiates the want for a physical connection. As our dating model states, the gathering of enough favorable information takes your potential love interest through the Bust-Down Worthy phase and thrusts them into the ...

Mental Bond Progression

Friendship phase: Here you begin to learn more things about your interest that aren't rooted in the superficial ideas of intitial physical atttraction. As you can see, at this point you're now building rapport to establish both the mental and physical bonds. Once you've gathered enough info and built rapport, you guys end up in the ...

Higher-Level (Spiritual) Progression

D8able phase: Right around here you guys have decided to be together, based on all of the info you've gathered and rapport building done in the previous phases. Ideally, this is where you both have reached the mutual want to build something long-lasting. The higher-level rapport building/bonding begins. At this point you're strengthening all three bonds.

As you can see, theoretically, once you've reached the D8able phase, you and your significant other would be fortifying the three bonds you need to sustain and grow a healthy relationship. We'll discuss this a little bit later, but it is important to note at this point that during the initial building of a relationship, the mental and spiritual bonds cannot exist without the physical bond starting everything off. Later on, you may see a relationship on life support because one or multiple bonds have been weakened, but initially, you can't have a full relationship without all of them.

Herein lie the reasons we're taught to abstain from sex in the early goings of this process. It is because of the potential for the physical bond you're creating to overpower the other bonds. Remember, the physical bond is potentially around a lot longer than the other two. It is continuously being strengthened right along with the other two bonds. As the other two bonds are being fortified, your physical bond is getting that much stronger as well. You best believe that at some point, you're going to want to give in to that physical connection, but the trick is to allow for those other connections to sort of catch up, if you will, with the ever-strengthening physical connection. To avoid ending up a fuck-buddy, if you don't want to be classified as such, or to avoid one-night stands, you need to build those other connections. Then when you finally do get to the physical intimacy, there's a much greater chance of you two ending up together. It's just a much more emotionally intelligent move to go this route.

Staying away from physical intimacy, namely the sex, allows you to get a better grasp of the other person without using clouded judgment. Oh yes, sex clouds judgment. Sex is that key to the floodgates that'll allow the physical connection to drown you if the other connections aren't present. Remember, physical connection has been developing longer than the other two connections. Sex too soon will place too much of the emphasis on just the physical connection. In worst-case scenarios, this can nullify the work you've done up to this point to create the other connections.

And the Self

The hot-and-sweaty encounters you crave can't happen without you. They shouldn't happen until you're ready for them. It is a stone-cold fact that the more comfortable two people are with each other, the more they'll be willing to explore in the bedroom. Our brains expend a lot of energy attempting to corral the emotionally driven actions of the heart. We innately understand how important it is to have an understanding of the person we're dealing with before we swap bodily fluids with them. Externally, dating manuals such as this one, dating consultants, and dating columnists stress the importance of being comfortable with someone before rolling around in the sheets.

Risk management, in terms of affairs of the heart, all has to do with fortifying oneself in an attempt to make the best decision when it comes to love and sex. To allow yourself to be at your most vulnerable with someone, you need to have a certain level of trust in and comfort with that person. We are all different. She may be comfortable a lot sooner than you, but it's a process that we all need to go through to protect ourselves in the high-stakes game of sex and love.

Comfort comes with time. But more importantly, comfort comes with exploration. First and foremost, you need to be comfortable with yourself. It has been stated throughout this manual, but again, everything starts with you. Self-understanding will create a smarter, more informed you in all aspects of life, as well as this one. Greater self-understanding will definitely grant you with a vastly improved ability to make decisions in regard to dating, relationships, sex, and love.

You also need a good understanding of your potential significant other. The approach you take to self-exploration is the same route you need to take with your love candidate. The more you know, the better. Physical understanding is one thing. Mental understanding is another. This is how the other person's insides work. This is their motivations. This is their passions and goals and all the little elements that help define them as an individual. Of course, you'll never have the grasp on someone else that you can have on yourself, but you can educate yourself as much as possible about your love interest. Yes, this will build a rapport between the two of you, but it will also better equip you in handling this person. You'll be more informed and better able to make the smarter decision when it comes to taking steps toward physical intimacy.

Finally, you need to explore how you two are together. Is the relationship one-sided? Do you both make serious efforts to consider each other? Are you the dominant person in the relationship? Maybe they are. Maybe you guys have the ideal relationship, where everything is equal. Whatever your respective setup is, the more you know about the dynamic, the more comfortable you'll be.

Understanding these three aspects of your relationship will help you become more comfortable, clue you in to the faulty areas that need work, or give you the information you need to prep for a run to the hills.

The ideal relationship can be illustrated as such:

All avenues lead to a happier, more open relationship. The more you know, the less you have to give someone the side-eye for acting irregularly. More importantly, the more comfortable you two get with each other, the more you can increase the scope of sexual things you'd do with, to, and for each other. You'll know you've reached that level of comfort when you don't have objections to sex. You'll also feel the readiness to explore different sexual activities.

Sexual Common Interests

For a safe start to sexual exploration, you guys should go here. Unless, of course, both of you are the sexual-adventure-seeking types, then by all means, let your imagination be your ceiling. Just like other common interests described in the chapter so creatively entitled "Common Interests," your sexual common interests can be used as your safety net—a sort of fallback, if you will, in the event that you guys don't agree on trying something new. You'll always have an established set of growing sexual activities to engage in.

As you guys begin exploring, clearly this list of sexual activities will grow. You two should strive to keep the sex fresh by trying new things. As an individual, once you're comfortable enough, you should continue to find things to melt your lover's socks off. They should be doing the same for you. Going out and finding something brand new to both of you is yet another way to discover something together. In essence, you should be treating your sexual exploration and search for new common interests in the exact same way you'd treat learning about your other mutual affinities.

That is, after you've established, in your mind, that you're comfortable enough to do so.

Timetables

Only you know when you're comfortable. Not even your mate can tell you that. If you're still on the fence, take that as a no. You're not quite there. People ignore their instincts when they really shouldn't. Once you've spent enough time, gathered enough info, and developed the relationship enough to your liking, you'll know when you're ready to get down. There's no sense in forcing anything. If the person you're dating cares about you, guess what? They're not going to mind easing on the brakes a bit to help you out. The truly caring person will want, above all else, for you to feel secure in this situation.

And if you're the one being pushy in the relationship, go sit down and rub a few out. There's no short supply of audio-visual stimulation out there. It'll mean a lot more to your love interest if you let them come around in due time. The sex ain't going anywhere. Yes, we all have urges, and yes, the allure to jump in bed with someone can have its own gravitational pull. Waiting will be worth it in the end. When someone feels like they've made a decision of their own free will, they're likely to be open to more. This is because there's no pressure behind their decision. They feel as if they have the power in making the decision.

Are you on someone else's timetable? If you feel as if the person you're dating is more worried about their gratification than your comfort, then you might be. If you're always going along with what your love interest wants, be it socially or sexually, you may be on their timetable. If you feel that this could be the dating life you're living, step back and look at things objectively. Ask yourself what role you're playing in the relationship. Are you guys equals, or are you the sidekick? If playing Robin isn't quite your thing, then you may need to communicate that to them. Please review the proper ways to communicate in the chapter titled "Communication."

Once everything is settled and you're ready to go, have fun. Let your guard down. Do what all of us are equipped to do.

The Pain of Sex

What is it about having sex early that's so dangerous? There has to be something to this, because so many dating consultants preach to stay away from premature sexual encounters with a potential mate. We all know what the supposed outcome will be. Nine times out of ten you'll get labeled a streetwalker, and get categorized accordingly: Bust-Down. Fine. Then there's the whole "dealing with feeling used" episode.

Those explanations do well in elucidating *why* we shouldn't jump into a bed so quickly, but they do not explain *why* there's such a sting if and when things go south.

Understanding the concept of waiting for sex until you've reached a certain level of trust in and comfort with your potential mate is not difficult. We've discussed this at length. Understanding why rejection or a failed attempt at a relationship can hurt so much more with sex involved is something people may not be too familiar with. Well, it all stems from that initial bond. This isn't the easiest concept to tackle, but let's wrap our heads around this one.

As you know, the starting point for initial attraction is that Superficial Spark we've talked about. You may also recall that physical attraction and the development of the physical bond begin before the development of the other two major bonds, mental and spiritual. Sexual attraction is rooted firmly in the physical realm, but is enhanced by the inclusion of the mental bond and sometimes even the spiritual bond later on. Not to mention the fact that we come from sex, there is something in us that craves physical intimacy. However, there is also something in us—well, most of us—that leads us to be selective in whom we decide to engage in sexual activity with.

Here's where things get a little weird. Our bodies desire physical, intimate contact, but we can be selective in whom we actually want that contact from. Think back to the superficial thought processes involved in attraction. Certain people just don't do it for us on a physical level. When we do come across someone we're attracted to, that superficial switch goes off in our respective heads (big and little), indicating we're attracted to them.

Now, we've learned to be more cautious in regard to how and when we get naked and do the do with someone. We try to safeguard ourselves from players. We try to fortify our physical attraction with a mental connection as well. We learn about ourselves, and how to read others, all so we can make the best judgment call in regard to when we should drop the undergarments. As much as we prepare, build walls, and fortify ourselves, nothing is 100 percent guaranteed . . .

No matter how much you prepare, you're never at a more vulnerable stage than when you decide to have sex with someone. Unless you're one of the dogs on the hunt, opening up and allowing someone to have sex with you means letting down all of your walls, and completely trusting the person trying to lie with you. You're believing that their intentions are what they say they are. You're believing there's a future. You're believing this person actually cares. Most importantly, you're believing in yourself in making the right choice at the right time with the right person to be vulnerable with.

As human beings, we have the ability to think on a higher plane than a lot of the other creatures inhabiting the Earth. We think that this higher level of thought can help us escape the physical world. But even though we think on a higher plane, we are of the physical world, and therefore are still affected by it. This is the reason physical vulnerability can hit us so hard when it's exploited. Sometimes the amount of mental preparation you undergo still isn't enough to guard you against the negative effects of a serious sexual mishap, like sleeping with the wrong person. The physical world is our foundation, and its hold on us is very powerful. All the things we go through in the physical world can affect us mentally, and spiritually as well. This is why when you allow yourself to be physically intimate with someone and things suddenly go to the crapper, the pain seems so deep. You're being rocked physically, but the effects are felt mentally and emotionally as well.

If things don't turn out the way you want them to, your world can experience a temporary toppling. Some people take this sort of setback harder than others.

Bonding

Your physical attraction may start things off with a potential mate, but it can take things only so far. Your superficial brain can think only so deeply . . . as in, on the surface. You need the development of that mental connection to carry your fledgling union to greater heights. If all goes well, you can achieve an ever deeper connection, as explained earlier. Reaching this point means you're pretty much in love and you guys are operating as "we" instead of "she and I." It takes the creation and growth of these three connections to get you to this point.

In order for your relationship to be fulfilling, you two would have to keep each of the three bonds healthy. And though these bonds are created and fostered at different points during your courtship process, after inception, they begin to find nourishment in each other. They sort of intertwine and feed off of each other. They can enhance each other.

Check this out . . .

Physically

Your physical bond feeds off your mental bond, and if you get to this stage, it feeds off your spiritual bond as well. Here's an example. Say you've been seeing someone for a while. You've always thought she is an attractive girl. The more time you spend with her, however, she just seems to grow more in beauty. Now, unless you guys have been dating since you were six, or she paid a shit-ton of money for plastic upgrades, her physical appearance hasn't really changed that much. It is your mental connection that is influencing how you view her. Maybe she does something really cute with her nose when she's explaining something she's into, or perhaps you've witnessed her sympathetic side. You're mentally registering these actions. They're being filed under the "stuff I like about her" section of your brain. Her actions, which have nothing to do with what she looks like, have made her more attractive to you. Because you've connected on that mental level, maybe you can appreciate her enthusiasm, or maybe you like the fact that she's a giving person, just like you. Whatever the reasons, they don't originate in how she looks.

Oh, and it probably goes without saying that a better mental connection can and usually means better sex. They say only a small percentage of what goes into amazing sex is the actual act of bedding. The rest of it is mental. When your lover takes the time to learn what you like, that's a mental endeavor. When they learn what things to say to get the two of you sprinting off the starting block, that's a mental effort as well.

The simultaneous building of a physical bond and a mental bond, if done correctly, will give birth to an emotional, spiritual, higher-level connection. For lack of a better term, let's just call it spiritual. The spiritual connection is something no one really understands, but people believe in it and you can definitely see the argument for it. If and when you reach a spiritual union with someone, your physical bond feeds off of this as well. That want to be around someone has its origins in the mental and emotional connections. Monogamy, for instance, is definitely rooted in the emotional and mental realms. The willfulness to sleep only with one person, to be physically intimate with one person, has to have at least some roots in a spiritual connection. They must've struck a chord somewhere inside of you to suppress that most human of urges . . . the want for sex from other people. If your physical bond isn't being nourished from the emotional side of your union, you may cheat. Who knows?

Mentally

Just as your physical bond is fed by its two counterparts, so does your mental bond partake in feasting on the positivity of the physical and spiritual bonds. At the risk of sounding like a famous kids' movie, your physical connection with someone, if positive, can have you thinking happy thoughts. This is serious business. When you spend time with someone, your body as a whole sort of adjusts to being around them in some way. Have you ever been with someone who made you really content and comfortable when you were around them? When you weren't near them, your brain was filled with happy thoughts and butterfly-like feelings coated your stomach. On the other hand, when you're around someone who tests your patience and makes you question just how flexible the term "violent" can be, you get a totally different feeling, don't you? Maybe your emotion has manifested itself as burning-hot needles in the pit of your gut. Even thinking about this person can generate an angry feeling inside. The thoughts you have about someone definitely correlate with how this individual acts with you in person. Their physical presence, along with the emotional connection you two share, can influence your mental connection with them. In good times, your mental connection with them will be enhanced. It's much easier to get along with someone when you actually like that someone.

Emotionally, Spiritually . . . Yeah, That One

All of the above. Let's just call it the other bond. This is the bond that can't quite be explained, but you know it when you have it. You know it's not a physical bond because this particular connection isn't tied to anything tangible. You know it isn't the same as a mental connection because there is no rigidity. This bond is sort of like the covering of a warm blanket on a chilly Midwestern evening. It's emotional security. It's an attachment of sorts. When you reach this bond, it's the glue that holds everything together. Can this be love? You're probably saying to yourself, "Enough with the Hallmark bullshit!" But those who have experienced this feeling know exactly what's being described. This feeling right here is the indicator that you're ready to be with that one person. Of all the bonds, it's the most symbiotic. It can't exist without the other two, and when it does exist it can enhance both the mental and physical bonds you've created. It's the cream filling to your Oreo.

When you're connected physically, mentally, and, err, spiritually, these bonds are a lot like the alternator and battery of a car. They work together to keep the relationship going. If one fails, the relationship will begin to stall. All three bonds need each other because each enhances the others. This is why when you see relationships struggle, you can pretty much trace the issues back to one or more of the bonds being weakened. In order to prevent this from happening, you and your partner have to be diligent in keeping the relationship fresh.

CHAPTER 12

SELF AND INDEPENDENCE

Do you know yourself? It seems like a simple question, but many of us do not. What's worse is that many of us don't realize that we don't have a real grasp on exactly who we are. Why is this? You say to yourself, "I've known me my entire life, how could I not know me?" True self-exploration (no, not of the sexual nature) is very rarely promoted in society. Though, some communities may look down on masturbation as well. Self-exploration is very rarely promoted by anyone, for that matter. Friends and even family members have their ideas of exactly who you should be. Did your mom want you to become a doctor? Maybe your best friend wanted you to follow her off to the same university after high school.

Society as a whole has a way of telling you exactly where you're supposed to fit based on race, gender, economic background, sexual preference, educational level . . . The list just goes on and on. The world isn't short on bird-minded people who willfully adhere to many of the categorizations. These same people will look at you sideways for trying to express an individualism that deviates from the norms, or challenges stereotypes that were set forth by someone who has no idea about your perspective on life in general. Other people have the audacity to express disappointment in what *you* decide to do with *your* life, what job *you* go after, or whom and how *you* decide to love. It's fucking insane. With these crazy zealots and hypocrites (who should be more worried about their own shitty existence) sticking their poop-smelling, judgmental noses in everybody else's business, it's no wonder that many of us don't even bother trying to figure out who we are and where we really fit into the world.

But, it is a developmental imperative that you do find out exactly who you are. Here's a hint: self-exploration never ends because we are ever-evolving beings. The real beauty of your internal journey is that fact. The fact that you're not the same person today as you were five years ago, five months ago, or even two minutes and forty-six seconds ago. True happiness is achieved only once you realize that it can be found only from within . . . and this ain't no silly greeting card colloquialism. It's absolutely true. Without internal acceptance, you may as well give up on attaining true happiness from any outside sources.

True understanding of self leads to joy, be it professional, social, or of love . . .

Self-Discovery

So, you've bought into the whole self-discovery argument. Well, how is it done? The first step is to free yourself from thinking that anyone other than you can have the answers about you. You may have been taking your cues from others in the past, but this is the time to take control over who you are. You need to develop a greater understanding of how you function socially out there in the world. Do you like being in the middle of it all, the center of attention, or do you prefer playing the cool, laid-back role? Are you typically shy, or do you ooze assertiveness? Self-discovery begins with a real look at your attributes, interests, and any and all of those things that define you as a person. Once you're clear on those things, you need to take a step back and develop a true appreciation for the building blocks of your character that make you unique. Becoming comfortable with your disposition and accepting your qualities are the first steps to being able to establish your place in the world.

All too often, we downplay our true characteristics. We wish we were different, that we could somehow modify certain elements of our makeup. Not just in the physical sense either. Yeah, yeah, magazines tell you that you need to be thinner. Media outlets may showcase someone who looks nothing like you and use them as an example of beauty. We're constantly being beat down, from multiple outlets, about how we don't look a certain way, dress a certain way, or walk, talk, and act a certain way. And while this constant barrage of reminders of our inadequacy can be a real confidence killer and overall pain in the ass, we downplay something far more important than our physical differences.

Many times we'll try to hide who we truly are internally and don these emotional costumes that we believe other people want to see. We perpetuate a false version of who we really are in order to fit in and not rock the boat. If we have attributes that deviate from what society views as normal, we view ourselves in negative ways. Too many of us have come to believe that our true selves aren't good enough.

So, for a true understanding of yourself, you need to reject those external banshees who scream to you that you're not good enough. You need to look inside yourself and realize that you're good enough for you and keep it moving. Really, truly believe it. If someone or some entity doesn't like you for you, that is not your concern. Mentally extend your business finger and push on, because you can't really explore who you are if you spend all your time hiding who exactly you are.

With acceptance comes growth.

Working on You

Remember that time when you asked someone out and they said something like, "I'm working on me. I'd love to go out, but I'm working on me"? You probably thought to yourself, "What a bunch of bullshit, you could've just said no." Well, now you have a chance to work on you, and it won't be an excuse to get out of exchanging numbers with someone, unless of course, you really use it as a reason not to share numbers with someone.

How does one truly work on oneself? It's quite simple, really. It requires a bit of honesty with yourself as far as who you are. Once you've uncovered the true you, you can engage in self-improvement. Remember all the stuff you were formerly suppressing about yourself? That's who you really are. Those elements make up the true you. Your likes, dislikes, passions, fears, personality traits—anything and everything you can think of make you who you are . . . And you're going to nurture every positive aspect of your character. You were given certain gifts. You have an affinity for certain things, and so on. Don't hide these things because you feel they won't be accepted. Be proud that you have talent in these areas. No one will support you if you don't first support yourself.

You'll set in motion ways to change the things *you* think you need to change, it should be stated again: you'll work on changing the things about yourself that you don't like. This isn't open for outside interpretation. Other people's opinions don't matter right now, just yours. You're going to have the opportunity to be selfish and enjoy it for once.

Also, realize that not everyone will like you. You don't need them to. If someone doesn't like you for the person you are, then you don't need to be dealing with that particular person anyway, in any capacity, be it professional or personal. You two obviously aren't compatible. Enough said. Don't dwell on previous failed unions. Learn from the mistakes you made, and strengthen your understanding of how you work within the world. Move on.

Passion Project

Let's start with the fun stuff. Say, for instance, you're secretly a comic-book nerd who would enjoy going to those huge conventions, but you never have because some arbitrary person looks down on that activity. You've turned over a new leaf, right? You don't care what other people are thinking, right? Right. You're going to go to the next local convention you can get to, alone if you have to. Some may think this is a silly example, but go with it. Everything will be revealed in the end.

Here's another example. You've always wanted to work for a not-for-profit organization that raises money for a good cause, but your parents frown upon it because you won't make very much money. No, you're not going to quit your job and run to the first job fair you see in the papers. Please don't quit your job. A smarter idea would be to utilize social media to find groups that are founded on the same passion that you have. If you can't find a group, create your own and recruit like-minded people to work with you.

Just because three examples look better than two, here's one more. You're really into musicals but none of your friends enjoy them. Go alone. You shouldn't put your passions and joys in the backseat just because you happen to have friends who don't share those same passions and joys. Before you get upset and look at the negative side of your friends possibly not liking the same things you like, view the very same issue as an opportunity.

How, might you ask, does one turn these seemingly solo excursions into opportunities for personal growth? Well, the actual act of exploring activities that foster your passions is a huge step in the right direction for your personal growth. Maybe you've been periodically flirting with your passions, or maybe you're removing them from the shelf and dusting them off. Either way, the more you engage in your passions, the more you learn about yourself locally, as well as globally.

Your passions are a lot like living, breathing organisms. The more you feed them, the stronger they grow. Internally, locally, your love for these particular positive things will be a source of contentment and joy for you. Also, by exploring your passions, you're taking steps to love yourself more, to better accept yourself and your place in the world. You are furthering your self-understanding.

Globally, tending to your passions can have an even greater effect. When you proactively seek out groups or organizations that promote your passions, you're opening yourself up to a subculture you may not have even known existed. This does a number of things. The first thing is that you're telling the world you're not ashamed of who you are. It's a positive affirmation that strengthens you internally and opens up the door for you to meet like-minded people, to be proud of your passions and stand with others who are just as proud. Another global effect of immersing yourself in groups that further your passions is that you increase your range of influence. Say, for instance, you've joined or started a fundraising organization that raises money for battered women. Your passion is going to fuel you to raise that money. It's going to fuel you to meet others like you. It's going to create a chance for you to do some real good in the world while simultaneously doing wonders for your psyche. The thing about yourself you previously hid from the world is now a shining example of what makes you a unique, and amazing individual. Not only that, you now have a support system that previously didn't exist. Finally, remember all those friends who didn't share your love of this particular passion? Well, you may be able to get them involved. If not, you'll make other friends who enjoy doing what you do.

In the grand scheme of things, as long as your passions are positive, nothing bad can come of you spending the time to nurture them.

Embracing Your Character

The characteristics that make you who you are should never be ignored, or suppressed, or modified to fit some mold other people have constructed for you. As long as these characteristics aren't detrimental to you or other people, they should be embraced. If you're naturally hyper, be naturally hyper. If you're an introverted, analytical bookworm, be the best introverted, book-consuming person you can be. Oh no, this is not to say that you shouldn't branch out and try other things. But, if you do branch out and add new aspects to who you are, make sure you do it for the right reason. The right reason is that you want to do this for you, for no one else but you.

Some people can't be the life of the party, nor do they really want to be. Some people are hardwired to be compassionate, while others are conditioned to lead. Embracing your personality and fostering your passions are the only ways to achieving true happiness. Remember, true happiness comes from authentic self-acceptance. Hiding who you are is frankly a waste of time and a pathway to discontentment.

Be objective for a second. Let's explore what true self-suppression and being socially fake actually does. The negative byproduct of this course of action can be much more socially stunting than the acceptance of your perceived outlier qualities. Denying who you are keeps you in a constant state of dissatisfaction. Why do you think this is? Simple. It's just like being in a one-sided relationship. You never focus on yourself, your real self, because you're spending all of your time trying to make someone else happy. In this case, you're spending all of your time living this pseudo-you existence in an attempt to coax social acceptance by pretending to be someone you're not . . . and just like a one-sided relationship, that shit is mentally as well as physically emptying. It's much easier to be yourself than to construct some quasi representation of what you *think* the world wants to see.

Turning Negatives into Positives

No one is perfect—not even Beyoncé, and she's damn close. Everyone has negative aspects of who they are that they can choose to try to improve over time. You shouldn't be down on yourself because of these things. You should take your weaknesses and try your hardest to transform them into strengths. In the process, you may learn something new about yourself.

Say you have a fear of public speaking, but you want to apply for a job that would require you to give presentations to high-level executives. It would behoove you to improve on the very weakness you have, right? You take a few classes and turn your fear into fuel. In the near future, you've practiced so hard that public speaking has become a skill for you and not a setback. Now you can go after the job you want.

This way of thinking can be applied to almost anything you perceive to be a negative in your life. Anger issues? Find an anger management coach who'll teach you ways to harness that anger and turn it into something you can use. Have you always been overweight? Do some research and teach yourself how to get in shape. If you can't do it alone, hire a personal trainer.

The point is not to settle. If you see something you don't like, be proactive about improving it. As human beings, we are not meant to be stationary. We are ever changing. A part of what it means to be human is to exercise the ability to think on a higher plane, thus establishing more control over our lives. The ability to figure out ways to manipulate outcomes in our favor is what separates us from any other species on the planet. You can be the master of your world. You get what you give. If you think and act positively, you have a better chance of getting positive outcomes.

Don't Pass the Buck

You have spent the past three or so pages reading a well-written argument conveying to you the importance of being proactive in shaping who you are. Taking full responsibility for the person you can be is the only option. Let's be totally honest here. No one, not even the woman who carried you for nine months and went through an excruciating ordeal to bring you into existence, has the ability to care about you as much as you can care for yourself.

Once you've made the choice to take your life and push it as far as humanly possible, you will achieve a sense of freedom, a sense of pride and power that can't be matched. Once you drill it into your brain that you are in fact the architect of your destiny, the stupid, vapid, external distractions that used to hold you in place have no hold over you anymore. What you once saw as insurmountable peaks become hurdles to be run over, around, or through. Make this realization, because the alternative is *much more depressing*.

The plight of the person who blames everyone else for their issues is a dark one. It is a downward spiral descending into a deep, dank hole with no hope of returning to the light. The sad part is, all this person would have to do is reach in their pocket, pull out a match, and light their way back to the top, out of the hole.

People who blame others for everything—seriously, everything—have in essence given up on personal improvement. As stated earlier, no one can possibly care more about you than you. Even if someone is to blame for a shitty situation you find yourself in, that someone isn't going to magically sprout a halo and two extra-large-sized wings and pull you out of the pickle they placed you in . . . They don't care enough. When you resign to sitting on your ass and blaming others instead of looking for your own solutions, you're effectively giving them power over you, a power, once again, that they will not use to improve your situation. Regardless of what the issue is, be it personal, professional, or something involving the heart, it is ultimately up to you to create the course that will lead you to where you want to be.

Don't allow yourself, mentally, physically, or emotionally, to be controlled by someone else. When you blame others for your problems, that is exactly what you're doing. The person you are—your passions, likes, dislikes, character traits, and more—should not be controlled by someone else. Your self-esteem and self-image in general should be a manifestation of the self-exploration you've done, not a foggy, one-dimensional background character in someone else's life story.

Do yourself a favor and reread the first three or so pages of this chapter. Work on self-acceptance, and eliminate the blame game from your mode of operation. People who love themselves don't have time to allow other people to control their happiness.

Self and Relationships

By this point, you're probably saying to yourself, "I thought this was a dating manual, not a self-help book." True knowledge of yourself and real acceptance of the unique creature you are both are imperative if you ever hope to succeed in a relationship. Knowing yourself is the true foundation of any relationship. Being successful in love totally ties in to who you are outside of the relationship. Your passions, your drive, your needs and your wants, even your interests and other elements of you make up who you are and determine not only who you'll be in the relationship, but also whom you'll attract and be attracted to. Once you have managed to accept yourself for the good and bad, for the uniqueness that is you, you're much more prepared to find someone else to love.

It is impossible to truly love another if you can't love yourself first. Why is that? Because the person you're going to truly love will be a culmination of passions, wants, needs, and character traits that both mirror and complement you as a person. The person you love will physically stimulate you, but more importantly, they would've made it through the dating phases and revealed to you that you two connect like children's building blocks.

This is why knowing yourself is so important. The more you know about yourself, the better the decisions you will potentially make when choosing someone to be your mate. As a matter of fact, the more you foster your passions, the better chance you have to meet someone with similar passions. This isn't empty advice. You'll naturally surround your-self with folks who have the same mind-set you do about any number of things. No spark blazes faster than the one between two people who already have major things in common. Recall the example given about working with the not-for-profit organization. You're bound to meet like-minded folks with similar interests just from submersing yourself in something you love. The chance of running across someone you can click with on an intimate level is exponentially increased because you're doing something you love.

Knowing yourself also includes understanding your strengths as well as your weaknesses in all realms of your life. These aspects of your self will also play a huge role in whom you're attracted to and whom you attract. Learn to play up your strengths as you begin to improve on your weaknesses. Remember, don't downplay these aspects of your nature, because ultimately you would want to attract someone who adores those particular parts of you. Improve on those things you consider weaknesses so they don't mentally hinder you during your social interaction with potential mates, as you escort them through the dating phases.

Confidence, true confidence, is developed by fully embracing the person you are. You are an ever-changing, ever-improving person with a lot to offer in a relationship. Cast-iron confidence can be developed only in this way. Confidence in oneself is a very attractive trait to have. People are often drawn to the person who doesn't care what others think about them. The majority of us worry about what other people think. A person who can separate himself or herself from this train of thought displays a sort of freedom that many of us wish we had. They also exude an attractive quality that's hard to ignore.

When You Fake

The want for social acceptance is a powerful thing, so much so that many times we try to adopt a persona that is not our own. We deny who we truly are as individuals in an attempt to be what society tells us we should be. The propagation of this quasi-fictitious version of ourselves is done for countless reasons, including—no, especially— to keep the interests of select people we have a definite intimate curiosity in. With the suppression of our true selves, it should be no surprise why countless relationship attempts never push off from the starting block, and why so many more burn out shortly after the initial sprint.

You can't expect to meet someone truly compatible with you when you're hiding your true self behind a projected falsified persona. Two roads emerge when taking your mate on this flawed journey: your new love interest will see through your smoke and mirrors rather quickly, and be turned off (which is probably the better outcome for you), or you'll actually be unfortunate enough to hypnotize someone with your costumed characteristics.

Make no mistake. This will be the start of greater issues. How long would you be willing to put your wants, needs, or passions aside? Can you actually suppress your true self, your likes and dislikes, for another person? Well, that's exactly what you will be doing once you decide to go with the "marvelous" idea to hide who you really are for the sake of impressing someone you think you want to be with.

Let's say you succeed in creating this sham "relationship." Remember, your new significant other has fallen for a phony, not who you really are. You won't be strengthening the bonds that build relationships with the new object of your affections, but instead your energy will be drained as you try to keep up the façade. The emotional and mental draining of trying to force a relationship to work with someone whom you really have nothing in common with is not worth the trouble. You may have a genuine affinity for this person, but their affections are misplaced because you didn't give them the opportunity to get to know the real you. You've managed to wedge yourself into a one-sided relationship, and you have only yourself to point the finger at.

The bottom line is that you've cheated yourself by not giving this person the chance to see who you could really be.

Lack of sincerity will lead to the premature death of your relationship because you choose to play a character instead of being honest. By modifying who you are and totally catering to your love interest, you're lying to them. You're masking the great person you really, truly have inside. What's worse is the lie you've continued to tell yourself. A happy relationship cannot be grown in the soil of a fake persona, watered with phony activity. This is why you need to be satisfied with your true self. No ifs, ands, or maybes.

Independence

It is clearly to be commended when people attain financial independence. This leads to physical independence, in most cases a child growing up and moving out of their parents' home. The importance of being an emotionally liberated person before entering a relationship cannot be stressed enough, but it is also one of those developmental issues that is often ignored. To be a truly autonomous person, one must learn how to be independent in all facets of life, including in love. The only way to reach this sort of liberation is by, once again, finding out who you truly are.

By this point, you've picked up the theme of this chapter. All things start with you, regardless of how you approach them. You can sit back and just let things happen to you, or you can take the wheel and drive yourself toward becoming the person you want to be. Self-improvement is definitely one of those areas in life toward which you need to charge head-on. You won't get better at anything by osmosis.

If you want to learn something, you read about it. If you want to improve in a sport, you practice. If you want to learn emotional independence, prior to entering the dating game, internal research is needed. Once you've reached that level of comfort with yourself, you'll be much more prepared to tackle the dating game.

True emotional independence is the realization that you don't need others to make you happy. *You* are your own source of happiness. If you love yourself first, then you'll be able to love other people.

A fortified relationship is often illustrated as the coming together of two halves to complete a whole. But, you also need to be whole within yourself. What this means is, you should be an independent individual aside from any unions. It is not uncommon for people to erroneously use their relationships and those they're involved with to define themselves. A solid, functioning unit requires the two people involved to be secure within themselves first. Then, the two lovebirds can define their relationship. The relationship does not, and should not, define them as individuals. A person lacking self-confidence and self-understanding will define himself or herself based on what the other person in the relationship thinks, or even based on the state of the relationship. This is a mistake because if all you have is your relationship defining you, it is bound to fail anyway. Your lack of self-esteem and personal understanding will syphon the life right out of the relationship you've created as you increasingly rely on it. More importantly, your partner will ultimately define who you should be.

Have you ever heard someone convey something similar to "He is my happiness" or "I don't think I could ever live without her"? Should anyone's opinion of you carry so much weight regarding how you feel about yourself? No. Hell no. Absolutely not. However, countless people's self-esteem is rooted in the opinions of others. Many times, these other people couldn't possibly know or care to know as much about anyone else as they know about themselves. No one can know you better than you. Therefore, you should look internally for acceptance instead of relying on outside sources.

Once you've learned to like yourself enough to explore who you are, you'll begin to understand the value of your uniqueness. Ultimately, the fostering of your passions, the honoring of your character, the showcasing of your strengths, and the acceptance and improvement of your weaknesses will create an unbreakable self-love. Your self-esteem will be rooted in what it should be: your confidence in yourself. Once you love yourself, it'll be much easier for you to love others.

D8ABLE LLC

D8able is a national LGBTQ psychological and behavioral match-making and relationship advising company based in New York founded by Tosin Adesanya and Tye Farley.

D8able is designed to teach the LGBTQ community how to be dateable before they attempt to include a partner in their lives. We educate on self and understand that self is the foundation to any relationship. There are steps to landing the ideal person and maintaining a relationship, but the first steps ultimately begin with the individual. D8able will help and assist the LGBTQ community, who genuinely want to meet like-minded individuals, to formulate meaningful relationships that lead to lifelong commitment.

The unnecessary taboo effects that have affected the LGBTQ community have caused generational stigmas, false understanding and beliefs that negatively impact the ability for many to formulate meaningful lasting relationships. This is where D8able comes into play. D8able has formulated a way for the LGBTQ community to meet and cultivate meaningful relationships through psychological analysis and genuine communalities. Instead of placing our focus on superficial meetings, we've gathered data through diverse forums that were held within the LGBTQ community and have found out what the LGBTQ community wants in a lifelong relationship. Our mission is to assist the needs of the LGBTQ community by hosting dating events, creating exclusive memberships, and fostering meaningful relationships that lead to lifelong commitments.

D8able works with professional psychological profilers who assist us with an array of objectives. First, they help us get to know our clients through the completion of our behavioral profile. During a review of the profile, our profilers identify strengths and weaknesses in our clients, which helps our clients get to understand themselves and the individual behavior that has led them to stay single. Ultimately, D8able believes that by understanding oneself, we give our client the comfort to invite someone else into their life.

D8able combines a total of sixteen years of professional experience. Our skill set ranges from people relations skills, psycho analysis, psychological profiling to crisis management. Within the LGBTQ community, there isn't a matchmaking company that provides the services that we do while targeting our clients in a psychological way, nor do they have the same skill range that we possess at D8able. Due to this, we believe that D8able has a tremendous competitive advantage against other matchmaking companies. It also provides us with the ability to add value and make a major impact on a community that is often neglected in this area of expertise.

Index